REVIVING TRADITIONS IN RESEARCH ON INTERNATIONAL MARKET ENTRY

ADVANCES IN INTERNATIONAL MARKETING

Series Editor: S. Tamer Cavusgil

REVIVING TRADITIONS IN RESEARCH ON INTERNATIONAL MARKET ENTRY

GUEST EDITED BY

TIGER LI

College of Business Administration, Florida International University, Miami, USA

2003

JAI
An imprint of Elsevier Science

Amsterdam – Heidelberg – Boston – London – New York – Oxford – Paris
San Diego – San Francisco – Singapore – Sydney – Tokyo

ELSEVIER SCIENCE Ltd
The Boulevard, Langford Lane
Kidlington, Oxford OX5 1GB, UK

CONTENTS

v

LIST OF CONTRIBUTORS

Chiang-nan Chao	St. Johns University, USA
Angelica C. Cortes	University of Texas-Pan American, USA
Dorothy G. Dologite	Baruch College, USA
Patricia M. Doney	Florida Atlantic University, USA
Eric Fang	University of Missouri, Columbia, USA
Steven W. Kopp	University of Arkansas, USA
Tiger Li	Florida International University, USA
Zhan G. Li	University of San Francisco, USA
Robert J. Mockler	St. Johns University, USA
Michael R. Mullen	Florida Atlantic University, USA
Saeed Samiee	University of Tulsa, USA
C. M. Sashi	Florida Atlantic University, USA
Charles R. Taylor	Villanova University, USA
Arturo Vasques-Parraga	University of Texas-Pan American, USA
Ka Zeng	University of Arkansas, USA
Shaoming Zou	University of Missouri, Columbia, USA

PREFACE

This special volume of *Advances in International Marketing* is devoted to international market entry issues. This is an important managerial decision in the internationally active company, and the papers featured here reveal new research findings. It is guest edited by Professor Tiger Li of Florida International University.

The idea for devoting a separate volume on international market entry originated from Professor Li. He issued a call for papers, which then attracted a variety of submissions of high quality. We owe grattitude to him for screening and evaluating these submissions, and for preparing the final set of chapters. We are also indebted to many colleagues who assisted in the review process. The resulting selections draw from a variety of perspectives and offer insights on foreign market entry and expansion issues.

Our thanks to Dr. Li for his efforts in creating this volume. Ms. Kathy Waldie, Managing Editor for the Advances in International Marketing series here at Michigan State University, deserves much credit for corresponding with the Guest Editor, the authors, and the Elsevier staff. Finally, we express our appreciation to Ms. Sammye Haigh, Mr. Neil Boon and other staff at JAI/Elsevier Science who saw the volume through the production process.

S. Tamer Cavusgil
Series Editor

REVIVING TRADITIONS IN RESEARCH ON INTERNATIONAL MARKET ENTRY

Tiger Li

INTRODUCTION

Over the last decade, market entry activities have continued to play a critical role in global economic development. In the transitional economies in China, Russia, and the Eastern European countries, newly emerged private enterprises, both large and small, have operated beyond national borders to build their wealth and social identities. In the developed economies in North America, Europe and the Pacific Rim, more and more companies have relied on joint ventures and direct investment abroad to relieve pressure from mature domestic markets. In the developing economies in Asia, Latin America, and Africa, governments have continued to embrace direct and indirect exports as a means to emerge from deprivation and poverty and participate in market globalization.

In contrast to the vibrant development in international market entry, extant research on the subject is running out of steam (Buckely, 2002). For example, countertrade, a major form of exports and imports, has grown to 15% of the world trade but studies on the topic have almost dwindled to naught. The practice of gray market has expanded to include everything from batteries and cars to computers and mobile phones. However, research on gray market, after a promising start in the 1980s, has become scarce. Research stagnancy does not limit to micro-marketing issues. The role of government in market entry has

Reviving Traditions in Research on International Market Entry
Advances in International Marketing, Volume 14, 1–8
© 2003 Published by Elsevier Science Ltd.
ISSN: 1474-7979/doi:10.1016/S1474-7979(03)14001-X

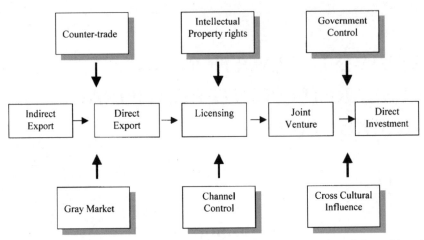

Fig. 1. Major Topics in International Market Entry. *Source:* Adapted from Li and Cavusgil (1995).

received little attention in spite of the active roles many governments, such as the Chinese and Indian governments, have played in creating a favorable environment to attract foreign direct investment and promote export. This is quite a departure from the Great Debate in international marketing literature in the 1980s over the role of the Japanese and Korean governments in creating an export-oriented economy.

This volume of the *Advances in International Marketing* is devoted to bridge a considerable knowledge gap between the practice of international market entry and the availability of research-based insights and principles for guiding that practice. Figure 1, which is an adaptation of a framework proposed by Li and Cavusgil (1995), shows some of the major topics in international market entry. Five market entry modes, from indirect and direct exports to joint ventures and direct investment, are illustrated in the middle of the figure. Traditionally, studies on these topics have exerted significant influences on the selection and maintenance of these entry modes. In this volume, each article addresses a particular topic in the framework. The first article (Samiee) discusses countertrade from a marketing viewpoint and introduces a unique marketing process perspective. The second article (Zou, Taylor & Fang) examines MNC's control in foreign investment by presenting and testing a model of government influences on MNC's control over its foreign market venture. The third article (Li & Li) develops a conceptual model of channel control in new product export and tests the model using data collected from the computer software industry. The fourth article (Mullen, Sashi & Doney) is a case study that highlights the complex issues in the gray market from the perspective of both manufacturers and parallel marketers. The next article (Kopp & Zeng) reviews the changes that have been made to Chinese patent laws and discusses managerial issues related to intellectual property rights. The sixth article (Chao, Mockler & Dologite) focuses on key issues for establishing strategic partnership between MNCs and their Chinese counterparts in the China market. The seventh article (Cortes & Vasquez-Parraga) investigates long-term marketing relationships in cross-cultural business using samples from the United States and Chile.

COUNTERTRADE AND GLOBAL ECONOMY

Countertrade is an umbrella concept covering a wide range of commercial mechanisms for reciprocal trade. Barter is the oldest and best known example, however others, such as counterpurchase, offset, buyback and switch-trading, have also evolved to meet the requirements of a more sophisticated global economy. All of these generally involve the exchange of goods or services to finance purchases, rather than using cash alone.

The pressure for countertrade in recent years has not abated as many predicted. When China and Russia initiated experiments in market economy, countertrade was the major mechanism used by the Chinese and Russian state-owned companies and private entrepreneurs in their cross-border trade. In the mid-1990s, following the collapse of the central planning system, countertrade flourished between the two countries and accounted for almost half of the bilateral trade. In Latin America, a new debt crisis has emerged as Argentina defaulted on the loans from the World Bank in 2002 and Brazil almost reached the default status. The new debt crisis has prompted a sharp increase in the amount of countertrade because the crisis has made ordinary trade financing more risky.

Samiee's article is a timely study that examines countertrade from a marketing viewpoint with a primary emphasis on the seller or supplier, but also from the buyer's or user's point of view. Based on information gathered through a literature search and personal interviews, the author introduces the concept of reverse marketing. The central point of this concept is the reverse sequencing of marketing processes, which, in turn, leads to many inefficiencies. Within the context of reverse marketing, a distinction between commodities and differentiated products is made. The analyses that follow suggest that, in the majority of cases, firms should engage in countertrade only as a last resort when it is absolutely necessary. Ideally, a countertrade transaction should provide financial returns that are equal to (or greater than) those of money-based deals.

GOVERNMENT CONTROL AND FOREIGN DIRECT INVESTMENT

Institutional perspective is a major stream of literature formed over the last two decades in international business and marketing research. It views government agencies as an institution and focuses on the role of government agencies in shaping economic and trade activities. In the 1980s, the literature focused its attention on the role of the governments in the Pacific Rim countries, including Japan, Republic of Korea, Taiwan, and Singapore, in promoting export and attracting foreign investment. In recent years, the interest has been shifted to the question of how governments in transitional economies, e.g. the Chinese and Russian governments, shaped a transition from a planned economy to a market-oriented economy.

Another major topic in the institutional perspective literature is the relationships between a host government and multinational corporations: what role a host government plays in framing the governance structure that is available to multinational corporations and the influence of host governments on MNCs in terms of the level of ownership and control over their foreign ventures. Zou, Taylor and Fang examine the extent to which host governments and their policies still influence MNC's equity stake and perceived level of management control. In order to examine these relationships, a model is proposed and tested based on the results of a large-scale survey of U.S. MNC executives. The authors find that host government preference does influence MNC's ownership control over its foreign market venture, which in turn influences its management control over the venture. These findings suggest some support for studying foreign market entry from a bargaining power perspective. While very specific restrictions may not have much impact on management perceived level of control, the government's preference often does. Thus, for MNCs, the host government's preferences still often play a significant role in management's equity, strategic, and operational control over the venture. Hence, even in this era of increased competition for investments and a more linked global economy, the host government's preferences still matter and theoreticians are well advised to weigh this factor in models of foreign market entry.

CHANNEL CONTROL AND NEW PRODUCT MARKET ENTRY

Channel control is an important issue in international marketing. At the upper end of the control system, a firm can establish a wholly-owned subsidiary in a foreign market and perform all the marketing functions itself in product distribution. At the lower end, a firm can contract an independent distributor and consign all the tasks of product introduction. In between, a firm may choose intermediary options such as forming an equity alliance with a foreign partner. These choices have a significant impact on product market performance because each level of integration offers a firm a different degree of control and capability in product entry in a foreign market.

In spite of the amount of research on this subject, several issues are not addressed in the literature. First, mature products have received much attention in previous research and channel control for new product export is not adequately examined. Second, among prior studies, few explored the impact of channel control on product market performance. Third, previous studies placed an emphasis on the effect of asset specificity on channel integration. However, their asset specificity was examined in the context of investment in service industries or general business and the findings are not readily applicable to investment in new product development in emerging industries.

Drawing on transaction cost analysis, organizational capability, and marketing control perspectives, Li and Li address these issues through developing a conceptual model of channel integration in new product export. They further test the model using data collected from the computer software industry. The findings indicate that both channel control and new product competitive advantage exert positive impacts on product performance in foreign markets. The results regarding asset specificity, country risk, and firm size offer interesting insights about the linkage between these antecedents and channel control.

GRAY MARKET IN THE NEW CENTURY

A gray market is an unauthorized distribution channel through which a manufacturer's genuinely branded product is sold at a reduced price to consumers. An alternative explanation is the unauthorized importation of goods into a market at a price lower than that offered by authorized distributors. In spite of the efforts from manufacturers to curb them, gray market activities have not subsided but have become rampant. Gray market products have expanded from traditional consumer products, such as cigarettes, cameras, and automobiles, to high tech products, including computers, cell phones, and networking equipments. These activities are prevalent in both developed and developing economies. For example, in the U.S., gray market products accounted for over $20 billion in revenue in information technology industries in 2001. In the emerging market of India, sales of more than 20% of computers and 70% of mobile phones occurred in gray markets in the same year.

Though past research on gray market products has laid a solid conceptual ground, empirical and case studies are still rare. Multinational firms are reluctant to openly discuss the specifics from their firm's perspective because of the strategic and legal issues involved. To address this void, Mullen, Sashi and Doney's case study highlights issues concerning parallel channels of distribution as an alternative mode of entry and helps readers evaluate theories using field observation. They gathered data from public records to develop a topical case study that gives students of international business and marketing a chance to analyze the creation of an international parallel channel of distribution from several perspectives: that of the manufacturer, authorized distributors in different territories, and the gray market entrepreneurs that attempt to arbitrage price differentials between the U.S. and European markets. Thus, students can consider a "gray market" situation as a threat or opportunity and compare theory and practice. The case also addresses the role of international trade shows as an important promotional aspect of international market entry. Finally, in their discussion and appendix, they provide information that is helpful to managers and students of international marketing.

INTELLECTUAL PROPERTY RIGHTS
AND THE CHINA MARKET

China has continued to receive much attention in the study of international business and marketing. From 1978, the year China started to reform its economy, to 2001, China's gross domestic product (GDP) increased at an annual rate of close to 9%. As China is transforming steadily from a planned economy to a market economy, many multinational corporations have converged in China, attracted by the prospect of reaching one-fourth of the world population with a newfound spending power. In 2001, China attracted the second largest amount of foreign direct investment, next only to the United States. Today, more than 80% of the Global Fortune 500 companies have established joint ventures and direct investment in the country.

Improvement in the protection of intellectual property rights is one of the reasons attributed to the rapid growth of foreign direct investment in China. However, changes in this aspect of China's legal environment have only recently received attention in academic research. In their article, Kopp and Zeng describe the creation and changes of the patent system in China and examine the effects of these changes and the competitive environment that they create on entry strategies into the world's most populous market. Their discussion first focuses on the enormity of the changes in China's patent laws that have been necessary for the country to gain access to the World Trade Organization. In seeking integration into the global marketplace, China has undertaken a series of legislative initiatives that brought the country's patent laws more in line with international standards. Then they examine the current business legal environment in China, with specific focus on the patent laws that are currently in effect, and discuss in detail the changes in patent activity since the institution of the new patent laws. While continuous efforts have been made to improve the protection of innovation, enforcement and litigation are still unpredictable. Finally, with this legal and competitive environment in mind, managerial recommendations with specific application to entry decisions into Chinese markets are provided.

CROSS CULTURAL BUSINESS AND COMPARATIVE STUDIES

As a result of market globalization, business relationships have become more and more cross-cultural in nature. Externally, a company needs to form relationships with customers, suppliers, distributors, and competitors of different cultural backgrounds. Internally, a company, particularly a multinational corporation or a joint venture, needs to manage relationships among employees, managers, and executives of diverse cultural backgrounds. Comparative studies are valuable because they provide insights into these cross-cultural business relationships and provide guidance for managing these relationships.

Chao, Mockler and Dologite offer a comparative study about establishing strategic partnerships in China. Because of the constraints on data collection, when conducting primary research in China, examination of strategic partnerships in China has been largely from the perspectives of the Western partners alone, or the Chinese counterparts alone. As a result, the research findings have been substantially one-sided. In their study, Chao, Mockler and Dologite attempt to overcome the bias and examine executives in MNCs and their Chinese counterparts in their partnership. How do MNCs and their Chinese partners view the foreign direct investment conditions in China? What are the partners' reasons for establishing strategic partnerships? The study reveals significant differences exist between Western MNCs' executives and their Chinese counterparts. The findings suggest that in order to succeed, joint ventures in China should largely focus on joint venture partners' marketing capabilities, and bridge the differences between the joint venture partners. They also advise MNCs to invest in technology, management know-how, and equipment in a venture partnership, and then source locally and market locally and abroad.

Cortes and Vasquez-Parraga's article investigates long-term marketing relationships in cross-cultural business in two contrasting cultures, the Anglo-Saxon and the Latin. Their paper intends to advance research on the identification and description of the primary steps that enable the formation and maintenance of relationship marketing. First, the authors focus on: (a) the communication processes, with emphasis on the set of social codes that govern business interactions and facilitate the generation and maintenance of long-term business relationships; and (b) the role of trust and commitment, two factors found to be prerequisites for establishing long-term relationships. Second, they develop the building blocks, or enablers, that are needed to generate and maintain enduring relationships. They finally illustrate the suggested process by describing the use of enablers in two contrasting cultures, the Anglo-Saxon and the Latin, using samples from the United States and Chile.

REFERENCES

Buckely, P. J. (2002). Is the international business research agenda running out of steam? *Journal of International Business Studies, 33*(2), 365–373.

Li, T., & Cavusgil, S. T. (1995). A classification and assessment of research streams in international marketing. *International Business Review, 4*(3), 1–27.

INTERNATIONAL COUNTERTRADE: A REVERSE MARKETING PERSPECTIVE

Saeed Samiee

ABSTRACT

Despite the proliferation of countertrade (CT) literature, it has not been examined from a marketing process perspective. *This study attempts to fill this gap. The concept of* Reverse marketing, *which is a direct consequence of CT, is introduced. A conceptual CT framework, which makes a distinction between commodity and differentiated products, is developed. The central point of this concept and, ultimately, of this article is that the reverse sequencing of marketing processes leads to many costly inefficiencies. The analyses that follow suggest that, in the majority of cases, firms should engage in CT only as a last resort.*

INTRODUCTION

PepsiCo, a firm recognized for its success in the Russian vodka-for-syrup deal, was unsuccessful in Romania because after the completion of the countertrade (CT) deal, it learned that its trading partner did not have sufficient capacity to produce bottles to ship its wines to Pepsi (Kassaye, 1985). It also learned, even after several price reductions, Hungarian shoes could not withstand the competition in the U.S. market from other imports. In fact, the success of PepsiCo's biggest CT deal, i.e. the Stolichnaya vodka as means of repatriating profits earned in Russia, would have been doubtful if the firm had not acquired Monsieur Henri, a wine

Reviving Traditions in Research on International Market Entry
Advances in International Marketing, Volume 14, 9–33
Copyright © 2003 by Elsevier Science Ltd.
All rights of reproduction in any form reserved
ISSN: 1474-7979/doi:10.1016/S1474-7979(03)14002-1

and spirits distribution firm.[1] These experiences illustrate inherent *marketing* problems associated with CT transactions.

Since the fall of the Berlin Wall in 1989 and breakdown of the Soviet Union in 1991, academic interest in CT has faded. There appears to be a sense that with the emergence of market economies in much of the world, CT has become an outmoded business tool of the past century. However, conditions that promoted the rise of CT in the world economy are very much present in many parts of the world and, as a matter of necessity, governments and firms find it necessary to engage in this form of doing business across national boundaries (Davis, 2002). There are reports, for example, that indicate that Western firms, at times as a matter of necessity, continue to rely on CT when doing business in developing and emerging markets (Damitio et al., 1995; Davis, 2002; Lo, 1995).

The objective of this study is to examine CT from a marketing perspective primarily as it pertains to the seller or supplier (typically a developed-country firm faced with CT demands), but also from the buyer's or user's point of view (the organization demanding or wishing to pay for products it needs with other products). The literature is almost void of CT analysis from a marketing viewpoint and the main objective of this paper is to provide an analytical framework for CT from this perspective. Concurrently, the *reverse marketing concept* is developed to systematically examine CT from the viewpoints of the marketing concept and market segmentation. Inasmuch as profit maximization is central to the theoretical underpinnings of market segmentation (Claycamp & Massy, 1968), performance resulting from CT is also central to this framework. As will be seen, from these perspectives, CT transactions make little sense, but since they are very much an instrument of international trade and have withstood the test of time, a model is offered to enable management to compare the profit expectations of CT deals with conventional transactions.

Since buy-back deals do not entirely bypass the price system (Rugman, Lecraw & Booth, 1986), the primary focus of the analyses that follow is CT transactions that exclude buy-back transactions.[2] In addition, emphasis is placed on the exchange of merchandise between developed nations and centrally-planned or developing countries. However, these arguments can be extended to include buy-back forms of CT as well as CT transactions among developed countries.

CT activities have received a great deal of attention in professional and trade journals over the last ten years. CT has been touted as one of the most interesting and important international business issues during the decade of the eighties (Lecraw, 1989). The existence of several publications (e.g. *Trade Finance, Countertrade Outlook, Countertrade Update*) devoted entirely to the coverage of this form of trade is a testament to the level of activity and interest in CT. Many major firms (e.g. Boeing, Cadbury Schweppes, GM, and Unisys) have established

CT departments to take advantage of countertrade opportunities available in the international marketplace.

The greatest increase in the number of countries engaged in CT occurred in the mid-1980s (Bussard, 1984b). A 1985 survey by the U.S. Association of Counter-trading Corporations indicated that 85% of multinational firms (MNCs) surveyed had received CT demands from a total of 65 nations (Carter & Gagne, 1988). A more recent estimate from the U.K. places CT-related volume of world trade between 5 and 40% (Davis, 2002). A natural response to the increasing volume of CT deals has been the creation of several new forms of channel intermediaries, such as CT consultants, switch-traders,[3] and merchant countertraders, who have risen to prominence in the process of accommodating CT transactions.

With the exception of a limited number of reports by the World Trade Organization (WTO), Organization for Economic Cooperation and Development (OECD), and International Trade Commission (ITC) which have criticized this form of trade (e.g. de Miramon, 1982; *U.S. Export Weekly*, 1982),[4] much of the writing on CT centers on its benefits, often promoting this form of trade as a way of entering a new market or increasing sales volume to current customers (e.g. Carter & Gagne, 1988; Elderkin & Norquist, 1987; Schaffer, 1990). The near-exclusive focus of the literature on the benefits of CT is evident in a review of advantages and problems associated with this form of trade. Carter and Gagne (1988), for example, offer a long list of references attesting to the benefits of CT, but offer only scant evidence, such as the "distinctly pejorative" titles of three trade journal articles, regarding problems associated with CT (Neale & Shipley, 1990).

A limited number of studies which have taken the middle ground position in the CT controversy have been written from trade theory and finance perspectives (e.g. Lecraw, 1987; Mirus & Yeung, 1986). Nearly absent from much of the writing to date is the rationalization of CT transactions from a marketing perspective and the inherent pitfalls of many countertrade deals. As noted by Lecraw (1989), data on CT transactions, particularly those leading to losses and those from the buyers' viewpoints are scarce.[5] Only one study was encountered in the literature that empirically assessed corporate profitability of CT. The study, sponsored by the National Association of Purchasing Management, showed that in the majority of cases (i.e. 68%), firms have either lost money or broken even in CT transactions (Bussard, 1983).[6]

To examine CT from a marketing perspective, a brief discussion of its rationale and relationship to marketing follows. Since CT is a very different form of exchange, it is also critical to examine CT from an organizational viewpoint. Then a brief discussion of CT volume and its role in world trade is offered. Next, the underpinnings of marketing and their relationships to CT are explored. In this context, the reverse marketing framework is developed and its elements are discussed in detail. Finally, an examination of market access and marketing know-how (common reasons for engaging in CT) and CT impact on corporate performance follow.

THE RATIONALE FOR COUNTERTRADE

Support for CT as an efficient vehicle for international trade is based on: (1) the conceptual treatment of CT activities; and (2) the assumption that both the seller's (exporter) and the buyer's (importer) resources *have alternative uses* (Mirus & Yeung, 1986). This rationale assumes that the global competitiveness of the bundle of benefits offered by CT merchandise is on a par with that of alternative products available in the open market system. However, the buyer's (importer seeking/demanding a CT transaction) alternatives for products earmarked for international trade are considerably more limited (or non-existent) than those of the seller. If this were not the case, there would be little incentive to offer merchandise as the buyer can use the open market system to raise the cash it needs to close the deal. This is an important consideration that has not been explicitly discussed in the literature. Such an analysis fills a critical gap in in CT knowledge.

By and large, CT is a rational reaction to pre-existing market conditions. From a conceptual viewpoint, these conditions consist of market information asymmetry, differential transaction costs, incomplete markets, and political and ownership problems (Mirus & Yeung, 1986). From a managerial viewpoint, CT may enable firms to increase sales and market share, enter otherwise inaccessible markets, and access necessary supplies. A popular argument for the use CT by many nations is the unavailability of foreign exchange. Countries with a good credit standing in the international financial markets, particularly those with an abundance of natural resources,[7] can typically access the needed foreign exchange to consummate monetary transactions. In other words, rather than shifting the responsibility for the selling of the commodities to be traded in a CT transaction to someone else, nations should sell these commodities and raise the necessary cash for the deal.

Typically, countries allocate their available foreign exchange based on their national priorities. Nevertheless, not every nation that requires CT is short of foreign exchange. Some choose to bypass the price system and demand CT to achieve other ends. For example, some foreign exchange rich members of OPEC who maintain excellent credit, use CT to bypass their allotted quotas at set prices, or to rid themselves of excess supply at close-to-established prices in saturated markets. Some have argued that, even among cash-poor, debt-ridden nations, the use of CT should be discouraged because CT reduces foreign exchange availability which is needed to repay their foreign loans (Suro-Bredie, 1983).

In a marketing context, CT is primarily a complicated pricing mechanism. Pricing decisions are influenced by many factors, including a firm's marketing philosophy, marketing plan, the level of competition, and corporate and brand image(s). Suboptimal decisions can result from uncoordinated pricing activities which, in turn, can negatively influence internal (organizational) and external (distributors, customers, etc.) resources and goodwill. Pricing or valuation of CT merchandise is one of the most serious problems for firms conducting CT (Cohen & Zysman, 1986; Neale & Shipley, 1990).

A CHALLENGE TO MARKETING PRINCIPLES

Marketing considerations constitute the most serious challenges in CT transactions and several studies have reported that the key problems encountered in international CT deals are marketing-related (Bussard, 1983; Neale & Shipley, 1990). In assessing CT transactions, three marketing considerations prove to be critical: market segmentation, market orientation and the observance of the marketing concept, and the organization of the firm.

Market Segmentation

The single most important consideration in assessing the suitability of CT from a marketing perspective is the economic theory that underlies segmentation and, hence, marketing theory. For most manufactured products, marketing thought has evolved from the microeconomic theory of price discrimination within monopolistic competition (Claycamp & Massy, 1968). This theory is the underpinning of the segmentation concept, i.e. the development and marketing of products to a homogeneous subset of customers with a distinct marketing mix/plan for each selected target market. Profit maximization for the marketer is then a function of pricing products in each segment in accordance with demand schedules in each (i.e. marginal revenue and marginal cost).[8]

Hence, CT fundamentally contradicts the methodical processes of planning and implementation advocated by marketing theory. Such contradiction, though not explicitly supported by CT writings in finance and international trade (e.g. Lecraw, 1989; Mirus & Yeung, 1986), is in line with their theoretical arguments.[9] The economic theory support for the rationality of CT transactions is based on the assumption that they create *net value* (net of marketing costs) in some form for all parties involved in the deal, and that the *value* received will *exceed* alternate feasible uses of resources allocated to such deals. Thus, the high marketing expenses associated with CT make it very inefficient from the viewpoints of efficient utilization of corporate, management, and particularly marketing resources, or profit maximization. Nevertheless, CT has the potential to *create some value for at least one of the parties along its distribution channel* and, therefore, is a rational economic reaction to a given set of pre-existing market conditions.

Observing the Marketing Concept

Another consideration in assessing the suitability of CT from a marketing perspective is the role that *the marketing concept* plays in and the extent to which *market orientation* is an aspect of the firm's marketing plans. Currently, the great majority of U.S. firms adhere to the principles of this concept which advocate satisfaction of consumer needs and wants at a profit through integrated marketing. The acquisition of products with undefined market segments (and, by definition, the absence of a prior marketing plan for these segments) through CT transactions necessarily leads to conducting marketing in a *reverse* fashion (i.e. product acquisition/development precedes customer need assessment and marketing definition). Since buyers typically offer unknown brands of merchandise in CT deals, reverse marketing presents serious problems as these products do not have well-defined markets.

Countertrade Organizations Within Firms

The third consideration in assessing the suitability of CT is the division of CT responsibilities within the organization. Since CT organizational structures vary considerably among firms, the identification of a locus of CT activities is essential in assessing the long-term profit picture. This is of critical importance because organizational expenses associated with CT activities must be fully accounted for and allocated.

The most common organizational format for conducting CT consists of maintaining in-house CT specialists within marketing or sales departments. There are several reasons for the popularity of this format. First, CT is not the primary choice as a vehicle for international trade for most firms. Thus, they do not want to invest or give the appearance that they are actively seeking this form of trade. Second, the costs involved in establishing a CT department may be prohibitive for most firms given their anticipated CT volume. Third, aside from requiring specialized knowledge and expertise, CT may be inconsistent with a firm's strategic objectives. Finally, some firms maintain CT specialists chiefly for internal purposes, i.e. to transfer funds (via goods and services produced internally) from one affiliate to another.

In some large firms, the responsibility for coordinating and consummating such deals is the domain of CT departments. CT departments are typically treated as profit centers with expected profits in *excess* of money-based transactions (to recover cost associated with CT) and return on investment rates (ROI) in line with alternative uses of funds. However, the expenses associated with assembling a CT department are prohibitive for the majority of firms and the marketing and/or sales departments which frequently provide the front line negotiation and planning efforts. Depending on their type and nature, CT deals may also involve many other departments (e.g. accounting, finance, manufacturing, purchasing). Even in the presence of a CT department, the marketing and sales staffs play critical roles in the eventual execution of the deal, and some CT departments (e.g. Combustion Engineering) serve only as facilitators for sales and marketing.

The type and nature of products and/or services received by the seller can vary from case to case. Thus, CT requires expertise that may be internally non-existent or inadequate. Even when such expertise is available, it can place extraordinary demands on various functional departments. Thus, in the majority of firms, resource allocation to CT activities is diffused throughout the firm and, therefore, *the actual costs of CT are not really known.*

THE REVERSE MARKETING CONCEPT

Reverse marketing occurs when firms attempt to sell products that have not gone through the traditional steps that are typically followed in introducing a product or brand to the market. This approach is analogous to the use of *the sales concept* which prevailed during the 1940s and early 1950s, i.e. the manufacturing of goods with little regard for the needs and wants of the segment(s) or market(s) for which they are intended.

From conceptual and managerial perspectives, both domestic and international CT transactions require a *reverse marketing* system. The reverse marketing process for CT shown in Fig. 1 requires that environmental assessment, the evaluation of customer needs and preferences, market segmentation, and demand analysis, which are the starting points for every sound marketing plan, take place after products have been designed and manufactured.[10] For example, demand for the product(s) that is (are) to be received in a CT transaction must be assessed at an acceptable price(s) with reasonable accuracy, and appropriate distribution channels

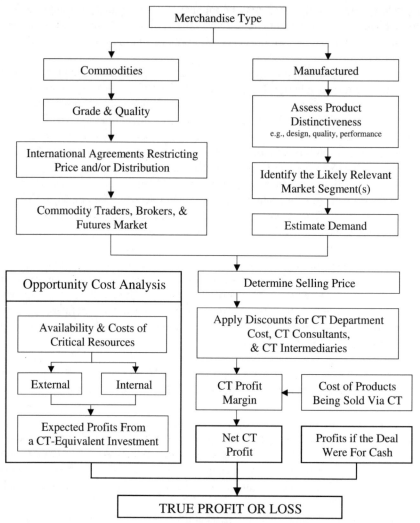

Fig. 1. Reverse Marketing in Countertrade Transactions.

have to be identified and cultivated. The fact that the firm might employ external resources such as switch-traders or CT merchants and consultants simply shifts this task to these intermediaries. Thus, aside from bypassing marketing fundamentals, CT transactions primarily place excessive pressure on two elements of marketing plans: pricing and distribution.

Technically, the exchange of products for anything other than money complicates the pricing procedure for both sellers and buyers. Sellers, in particular, are often placed at a distinct disadvantage because the valuation or pricing task for the merchandise or services to be received, their timely distribution, and spoilage and other risks associated with them become their problems. In fact, the pricing task may become so complicated that in the end neither party knows what they received *or* paid (Cohen & Zysman, 1986). Not surprisingly, Neale and Shipley (1990) found that pricing was among the top five problems associated with CT transactions. In addition, marketing costs (including the costs of direct use of various departments and CT intermediaries and consultants) associated with the CT itself must be estimated and worked into the price. However, this task becomes so involved that most firms, either by choice or default, do not take such indirect expenditures into account. A survey by the National Foreign Trade Council Foundation showed that 52% of the firms involved in CT had failed to include even the more direct costs of disposing of goods in their prices (Bussard, 1983). Information gathered from firms in this study indicates that, with minor exceptions, firms do not maintain adequate systems of assessing their CT transaction costs. Even worse, the costs associated with failed negotiations are never written-off against (or spread across) those that are consummated.

It is then apparent that the pricing of CT transactions is the critical starting point in assessing the profitability of a particular deal. However, a distinction between the valuation process for commodities and differentiated products should be made. Commodities and certain other homogeneous products generally have established market mechanisms on a domestic or global basis. Manufactured CT products from LDCs and centrally-planned economies often lack brand identity, but are aimed at filling specific needs and, by definition, are intended to serve distinct market segments.[11]

Deals Involving Commodities

Most commodities such as oil, cotton, and steel are homogeneous products for which there is existing global demand. The presence of various domestic and international commodity markets makes the pricing task for CT transactions involving such merchandise a relatively easy one. Therefore, it might be argued that the pricing of commodity-based CT deals is, by and large, not problematic. Frequently, buyers (usually a government agency) use CT as a vehicle to bypass limitations imposed by international commodity agreements. Saudi Arabia, for example, bartered crude oil at 10% below market prices for Boeing jets (*Financial Times*, 1984). Through this deal, Saudi Arabia both surpassed its OPEC production quota and disguised price-cutting. The 10% discount was necessary to defray additional marketing expenses for Boeing. In another CT transaction designed to bypass OPEC quotas, Saudi Arabia agreed to pay the British Ministry of Defense for 132 aircraft by providing 300,000 barrels of oil per day. Falling oil prices extended the terms of payment and, to avoid delays in the delivery of the aircraft, Saudi Arabia was forced to borrow $1.5 billion (James, 1986). However, there are few suppliers of military hardware which generally results in better CT deals for them. CT transactions involving non-defense products often result in a net discount (vis-à-vis monetary deals) to buyers as demonstrated by a CT deal involving Honda. In an effort to bypass the depressed oil prices, the Algerian government sought to make a deal with Honda using their higher official export price. Honda eventually agreed to accept 40% of the contract in oil at official prices excluding CT expenses, resulting in a 5.5% discount to the Algerian government.

As shown in Fig. 1, the valuation of deals involving commodities as payment requires a two-level screening process. First, an assessment of the grade and quality of the commodity *using international or Western standards* is needed. For example, cotton from LDCs used in CT deals may meet the required staple measures but not the moisture content which can affect weight. Even when the cotton meets both requirements, buyers have found a significant amount of foreign material in cotton gins, thus requiring further processing. Second, the supplier must have (or acquire) a working knowledge of numerous commodity agreements and market orders aimed at stabilizing world commodity prices. These agreements are at the mercy of world economic and political conditions. In particular, future delivery and prices of commodities covered by such agreements can be uncertain. Consider the experience of General Electric in a CT deal involving Kenya whereby GE received coffee beans in exchange for X-ray equipment. After the deal had been closed, the firm discovered that the value of the non-quota coffee involved in the transaction was only 50% of the anticipated market price. Also, consider the implications of having signed a long-term CT deal involving coffee just a few years ago. Following the collapse of the International Coffee Agreement, the market price for coffee plummeted.

With the exception of situations when a CT commodity is intended for internal use, the next stage of the valuation process involves commodity traders, brokers, and/or the futures market. To seek protection from fluctuating prices, the supplier or other intermediaries can buy protection in the futures market for a price, generally for periods of up to six months. Long-term delivery of CT commodities is nearly always problematic for the supplier (or the intermediary accepting the obligation) – hence its critical role in the pricing procedure. The value of transactions for periods exceeding those which can be protected through the futures market must be discounted based on present prices. If the terms of the transaction call for the delivery of goods over a period of years, pricing becomes an impossible exercise unless the CT transaction is open ended (e.g. Saudi Arabian deal with the British Ministry of Defense). For example, petroleum prices, as with many other basic commodities, will be difficult to predict with any level of accuracy because political and economic variables of supplier and user nations are in a constant state of flux. Futures markets can be helpful for short periods, but there is a cost attached to any coverage obtained through such mechanisms. A close-ended CT deal concluded in the late 1970s involving petroleum or petroleum-based products as payment over an extended period of time would have worked out significantly in favor of the seller. The same deal following the sharp drop in petroleum prices in the early 1980s might have caused the firm to go bankrupt.

Deals Involving Differentiated Products and Services

Manufactured products and services, whether industrial or consumer, can often be differentiated vis-à-vis existing competitors along one or more dimensions.[12] Estimating prices is considerably more complicated for this category of goods and services than for commodities. The complexity of the task is fundamentally tied to the *reverse marketing* character of CT transactions. Typically, differentiated products and services are conceived, designed, and manufactured for specific market segments with known characteristics and are marketed with specific marketing plans and resource commitments. In contrast, market segments for merchandise received in CT deals, particularly consumer products, are unknown. Lack of customer awareness and/or brand identity and penetration, as well as non-existent test market data, limit the ability of the seller or CT channel member to price the product(s) in question with any degree of certainty.

Firms receiving differentiated products in CT transactions must first determine the nature and market value associated with their distinct characteristics (e.g. design, quality, performance, aesthetics). This process is shown in Fig. 1 and may involve extensive ex post facto market research and is both time consuming and expensive. The need for the seller to carry out the market research responsibilities of the buyer has been stressed in the literature (Rabino & Shah, 1987). The seller, in addition to identifying and satisfying its own relevant market segments, must conduct market research to identify potential market segments for CT products it receives in exchange (i.e. a dual marketing role). Once the firm has successfully assessed the differentiating attributes of CT products and potential segments are identified, its biggest hurdle is estimating demand for the product.

Estimating Demand

In the absence of existing market mechanisms, accurate demand estimates for manufactured products are necessary to determine price and are critical in assessing the profit potential of CT transactions. Though demand level and price are inherently related, manufactured products technically appeal to specific segments of the market in which versions of a product are offered at a range of prices. Thus, as shown in Fig. 1, two critical aspects of assessing demand are segment identification and the determination of air market price(s). Estimating demand for differentiated products aimed at particular segments of the market (i.e. sold in monopolistically competitive markets) through a *forward* (normal) marketing process is the same as that in *reverse marketing*. However, accurate estimates for CT products are difficult to obtain because relevant segments are identified after the firm comes into possession of CT goods, though some estimates may be possible while negotiations are in progress.

Among other things, demand and, hence, price, are related to the firm's investments in marketing effort, brand identity, and position. In this light, assessing market potential for CT merchandise presents an even greater challenge. A major source of error in estimates of demand for unfamiliar brands, which are the likely candidates for CT transactions, is the lack of awareness in the channels of distribution and the accompanying absence of an established position for the product/brand. Brands that lack identity have undefined segments and positions, leading to uncertainty regarding their market potential and actual demand. Therefore, major concessions, e.g. deep discounts, promotional allowances, and incentives, would be needed to overcome these problems. According to one estimate, discounts necessary to overcome marketing hurdles in CT deals can be as high as 33% of comparable open-market ex-factory prices (*The Economist*, 1985). Some governments openly admit that higher prices resulting from requiring or demanding CT deals are no longer relevant (Davis, 2002). These realities, in turn, perpetuate the difficulties in CT transactions since estimates of market potential and, hence, marketable prices are necessarily complicated.

Uncertainty regarding time demands inherent in completing CT transactions is a critical element in assessing demand. Bussard (1983) reports that 54% of transactions involve more than six months of negotiations and the time needed for 24% of these exceeds one year. Furthermore, negotiations may not end on signing a contract. After three years of continual negotiations, Foxboro Company found it necessary to continue its negotiations for an additional two years (Kassaye, 1985) after it had signed a contract. Not surprisingly, Neale and Shipley (1990) found that the time required for CT negotiations was the second most important problem for British firms engaged in this form of trade. Thus, even if accurate estimates of demand for CT products were possible, by the time negotiations are completed they may no longer be valid. This leads to uncertainty regarding the timeliness of CT merchandise and, hence, the opportunity cost associated with CT deals. Fashion apparel, for example, is relatively short-lived, and must be available in abundance during its peak popularity. Delivery terms spanning six months or longer will not address market and marketing needs in Western countries. Increasingly, powerful apparel retailers, such as The Limited, test-market their products in a few stores before their national introduction. Once a design has been successfully test-marketed, they order, receive, and distribute the apparel nationally in as little as 30 days. Unless immediate capacity can be purchased from switch-traders, typical CT transactions cannot meet the needs of such firms.

Since brands are used as surrogates of product benefits, the lack of brand identity in CT merchandise further complicates the assessment of demand. Even in the case of industrial products, brand identity provides important quality and on-time delivery cues for buyers. In order to be competitive in the global market, firms rely on these elements. Reliable delivery terms, for example, are necessary prerequisites to using the increasingly popular just-in-time manufacturing method. Uncertainty regarding high and consistent quality and delivery makes demand analysis difficult and constitutes a major hurdle in CT transactions.

Countries that typically demand or require CT deals are typically LDCs and emerging economies whose products are often of inferior quality to effectively compete in Western markets. Even firms experienced in CT have great difficulty assessing the demand for CT merchandise. The experience of PepsiCo with Hungarian shoes referred to earlier (Kassaye, 1985) resulted from their difficulty in assessing product demand. Even when the price was reduced, the shoes could not compete effectively with other imports selling at much higher prices.

Despite these hurdles, the demand for CT products can be estimated in several ways. The most robust estimates are likely to result from test-marketing using scientifically acceptable techniques. However, other less-involved methods may be used as general guidelines. For instance, assessment of the demand for an existing product with similar attributes and market position can provide a guideline for expected market potential for a CT product under consideration. Inherent in this estimate is the expectation that similar marketing support will be provided for the CT product.

Determining Fair Market Price and CT Profits
The determination of an acceptable selling price is a critical step in assessing the profitability of each transaction. Once the appropriate market segment for CT merchandise has been isolated, demand level and expected *selling price* can be determined.[13] As shown in Fig. 1, the expected selling price should be reduced by the customary distribution channel discounts as well as other direct and indirect

costs associated with the CT department and/or personnel, intermediaries, and/or consultants. Ideally, the value of the CT deal after discounts and reductions should be equal to or exceed the firm's customary revenue in a monetary transaction, i.e. the firm maintains or improves its profit margin without deference to opportunity costs. Profit potential similar to that of conventional transactions is the single most important consideration in assessing the suitability of CT deals. In a survey of CT transactions by Bussard (1983), only 32% were shown to result in a profit for the sellers, one-half broke-even, and 18% lost money. Given that the information gathered for this study indicates that sellers do not fully account for the direct and indirect costs of resources allocated to CT activities, the proportion of CT transactions losing money as reported by Bussard is likely to be under-represented.

CT Opportunity Cost

As with other corporate resource allocation decisions, the decision to engage in CT deals should be based on *the expected return* from the best alternative use of resources. Resources expended to CT activities should produce the same ROI as other form of new investment by the firm. This concept, shown in the lower-left side of Fig. 1, is fundamental in the determination of *true* profits.

Short-Term Considerations
From a seller's perspective, knowledge of the resources utilized in CT (i.e. CT investment) is critical in optimizing its return. With this knowledge at hand, firms can allocate their resources more efficiently. For example, is it costlier to expand in a growth market or to immerse in CT transactions? Would it be more expensive to idle production facilities or to keep them running and possibly accumulate and carry an inventory until a CT deal has been consummated? Answers to these questions will depend on such factors as firm size, corporate strategy, cost structure, rate-of-return from conventional businesses, alternative uses of resources, competitive intensity, industry traditions, global trade and economic atmosphere, etc. Thus, detailed information regarding the firm's non-CT business activities should guide the assessment of financial feasibility of CT deals. Providing generalized answers to these questions is further complicated by the fact that each CT deal varies from others in its potential profitability and risks. Nevertheless, prior to finalizing a CT transaction, a firm should compare the rate-of-return from a CT deal with the expected return (using a full-costing approach) from alternative uses of resources.

Long-Term Considerations

Quite apart from the direct CT costs and benefits to the firm, there are indirect costs and benefits associated with the fit between CT and the corporate mission and objectives. If CT transactions are the only avenue for entry into certain markets, can they be considered windows of long-term opportunity? On what basis should they be screened? And should the firm exploit this mode of market entry as a matter of policy? Should MNCs engage in CT in order to preserve their market share? Some CT proposals request competitive bids from potential suppliers. Would it be desirable to engage in a bidding war against other U.S. and foreign MNCs, despite the many uncertainties involved in CT? Inasmuch as CT transactions vary considerably from one another and given numerous firm-specific considerations, generalized answers to these questions are not possible. Typically, the great majority of CT deals are not avenues for long-term market entry, but a few may qualify as such. In most situations, CT deals tend to be close-ended (e.g. Pepsi's syrup-for-vodka deal) and prevent firms from pursuing their strategic goals (e.g. the addition of new product lines and horizontal and/or vertical market expansion). Thus, if the firm lacks significant experience abroad (e.g. the CT deal is the firm's first opportunity to expand internationally), it is well-advised to avoid this form of market entry. On the other hand, if the firm has a broad-based international experience, it should use its standing policies to assess CT opportunities as vehicles for market entry.

Published CT data are both incomplete and fragmented and do not provide an adequate basis for exposing detailed answers to the important questions outlined above. Information gathered through interviews for this study suggests that most firms engaging in CT do not have policies on these critical issues. Thus, they handle CT demands and requirements on a case-by-case basis. Firms with a distinct image, differentiated products, and a reputation for high quality products and services generally have an advantage in bidding situations. As a matter of policy, some firms neither seek nor encourage CT involvement. IBM, for example, reportedly avoids CT deals (Cohen & Zysman, 1986). As a testament to this policy, the former Soviet regime frequently demanded CT in most purchases. However, IBM signed one of the industry's largest contracts ($20–$30 million) for computer equipment using a convertible-currency as the payment method (*The New York Times*, 1990b).

A survey of a dozen trading companies and consultants with specialization and diverse experience in CT also indicates that firms *do not* make an effort to determine the level of resources allocated to CT activities. Thus, they have no information regarding their ROI for resources earmarked or used in CT. It then follows that alternative uses of CT resources are not examined. Admittedly, this knowledge gap is difficult to assess because it occurs over long periods (the McDonald's deal in Russia reportedly took 10 years and the PepsiCo arrangement took around 5 years to negotiate), many deals are never consummated, and as noted earlier, resources deployed are generally diffused throughout the firm even when a CT department is present. Despite its critical importance, CT opportunity cost analysis is a difficult task unless provisions for reporting CT-related costs and expenses are made throughout the firm.

Firms without prior CT experience can expect indirect expenses associated with such deals to be at least equal to, but generally greater than, the typical CT consultant's fee for consummating a deal, i.e. "success fee." Consultants' customary success fees are about 8% but vary depending on the size of the transaction, nature of the product, and his/her relationship with the firm. In situations where CT products offered by the buyer are within the sellers' areas of expertise, much greater use of internal resources may be made and payments and discounts to CT intermediaries may be avoided. In any event, all individuals and departments that are likely to assist with CT transactions should report their CT-related time and expenses. Firms with experience in and exposure to CT transactions can measure direct and indirect resources and revenues allocated to CT activities over a one-year period so that a CT rate-of-return can be computed.

The presence of a CT department or a trading subsidiary and/or the hiring a CT consultant somewhat simplifies the determination of resources allocated. CT department costs are budgeted and known. This sum represents the firm's resources used for CT and should be proportionately allocated to all CT deals completed, thereby reducing their respective profits. Ideally, these cost allocations represent additional markups that the firm should add to its customary selling price to maintain its profit margin. Clearly, the opportunity cost of bypassing alternative investments should also be examined to see whether a better return can result from non-CT activities.

MARKET ACCESS AND MARKETING KNOW-HOW

Classical CT arguments of (forced) access to markets and distribution channels seem almost irrelevant in an era of global markets, information technology, telecommunications, and transportation. Although advances in information technology will lower CT costs, this is a two-edged sword since the customer demanding to engage in CT can use the available technology to sell its products and use the proceeds to complete its purchase. Receiving products in which a firm has no expertise and which are of unknown quality and brands is not a desirable avenue for buyers to access markets. Though information asymmetry, i.e. lack of business and marketing information and know-how, may explain the reasons for certain CT deals, many such transactions involve large (state) enterprises with direct access to needed information. Various export development models suggest that serious contenders in international trade eventually overcome information asymmetry regarding markets (Aaby & Slater, 1989).

If the products offered by the buyer in a given transaction are of marketable quality, i.e. sufficient distinction to become and remain competitive in the international marketplace, then there are existing indirect and direct distribution networks that can assist the buyer with distribution functions (export management firms, export trading firms, wholesalers, retailers, etc.). Having mastered the conceptual underpinnings of marketing and the perils of reverse marketing, the manager should also assess a CT deal in light of the buyer's circumstances, including his/her motives for bypassing the open market system. If information asymmetry is thought to exist, then the manager's task becomes one of providing market information and contact with appropriate (non-CT) intermediaries. Utilization of specialized CT intermediaries (e.g. switch-traders, barter agents) facilitates distribution of CT merchandise but is more expensive.

Most supplier firms are specialized in relatively narrow markets and do not have the expertise or the access to appropriate distribution channels for product(s) the buyer wants to CT. In non-buy-back CT deals, chances are that the seller has little or no expertise in the products included in CT. Hence, the marketing department has to rely on other groups (e.g. purchasing, finance) and such external resources as CT consultants and channel intermediaries to assess market potential and price, determine appropriate distribution channels, and promote and sell CT products.

Purchasing personnel are a knowledgeable source of information on possible distribution networks as well as prices for many, *but not all*, products. Furthermore, their main concerns revolve around the needs of the subsidiary or division they service. For example, the needs and, hence, the expertise of purchasing personnel at GE Medical Systems division are not identical to those at GE Aircraft Engines division. Naturally, the larger and more diversified firms are better equipped for determining distribution possibilities. Nevertheless, purchasing professionals are not in a position to estimate market demand for products that do not have established brands and, therefore, a market, or are considerably different than current offerings. Once appropriate channels have been designated, the firm must find a way of marketing CT products to channel intermediaries. The presence of additional members in the distribution network, be it the seller (the firm receiving a CT offer) or existing CT intermediaries, contributes to a more cumbersome and less efficient distribution system resulting in higher prices or larger CT discounts.

A distinction must also be made for products and services with a proportionately small or negligible variable cost. Providers of certain services, such as airlines and hotels, are in a position to consider CT as a viable alternative to acquiring products and services that are internally needed and that they must pay for. The marginal costs of unsold airline seats and hotel rooms are relatively small for their providers.[14] These "unsold" services can then be sold at substantial discounts in exchange or as partial payment for goods and services these firms need. Naturally, the selling and buying functions will become more complicated and expensive, but presumably, the deep discounts involved will make such CT transactions worthwhile.[15] Nevertheless, research has shown that a very difficult problem associated with CT goods offered in a transaction is to find an in-house use for them (Bertrand, 1986; Neale & Shipley, 1990; Shipley & Neale, 1987).

CORPORATE PERFORMANCE
AND COUNTERTRADE

The primary corporate performance criterion is meeting rigorous financial objectives outlined in the firms' strategic plans. CT transactions must be transformed into monetary transactions so that corporate performance can be assessed. CT credit through switch-traders and CT merchants is quite common and complicates the transformation of CT transactions into cash. Therefore, by definition, the realization of corporate objectives is delayed by CT because it reduces the time utility of corporate funds, increases risk, and places additional demand on various departments and functional groups. CT deals also make it more difficult to assess individual and divisional performance. Another problem arises from the scale of CT credits and obligations of U.S. firms. Estimates suggest that some major U.S. firms have accumulated obligations exceeding $1 billion in *non-commodity* products from LDCs and emerging markets. It is quite possible that the books of many firms engaged in CT collectively include dubious assets of colossal proportions (Cohen & Zysman, 1986). The Pepsi deal with Russia, for example, was worth $300 million in 1989, but Stolichnaya vodka produced only $156 million (*The New York Times*, 1990a). The remainder has become CT credit that the firm is attempting to balance by paying for the expansion of the firm's other businesses in Russia (e.g. at the time, Pizza Hut restaurants) and by involving itself in sales or the lease of a product category in which it has no expertise: Russian tanker ships. Everything else being equal, local use of non-repatriated funds represents an endless cycle that leads more CT credit.

There are other grounds for a firm to substantially limit or avoid CT transactions. Because of the organizational, marketing, and financial hurdles that must be overcome, CT deals generally require far more time and corporate resources than conventional transactions and, hence, they are more expensive. The cost and likelihood of failure of reverse marketing of CT merchandise are significantly higher than industry averages. Therefore, CT should not be considered a firm's primary vehicle for selling either domestically or internationally. Aside from the diseconomies that CT perpetuates, it may set a precedent with current buyers for future transactions, thus circumventing otherwise conventional deals. Given the status of CT in world trade, there are situations in which CT can be a reasonable marketing vehicle. However, as the seller simultaneously becomes a purchaser in CT, the marketing manager needs to proceed with extreme caution.

It is also important not to overstate the capabilities of internal corporate resources. For example, materials management or purchasing departments are not experienced in sales and should not be viewed as distribution or CT experts. Only 11% of the Fortune 500 firms involved their purchasing departments in selling merchandise received in CT deals. For the great majority of firms lacking a CT department, marketing departments are in charge of finding markets for the firms' products and services. They are the loci of marketing know-how and thus best qualified to take the marketing initiative.

AN APPROPRIATE ROLE FOR COUNTERTRADE

Given the bimodal distribution of economic wealth of nations, there is a consensus that CT transactions are here to stay, grow in size, and remain an important form of international trade for many years to come. The great majority of countries of the world are economically weak which are broadly classified into the developing group. Even the so-called emerging nations are facing significant economic difficulties. Within the last few years, several key "emerging nations" have been on the brink of economic collapse, e.g. Southeast Asian nations, Argentina, Brazil. It is thus fair to expect that, at the very least, the great majority of these nations will require some form of CT for their public procurement and projects.

Thus, many companies can expect to face CT demands, some of which may represent good opportunities for the right firm. The reality of market information asymmetry provides profit opportunities for firms interested in CT transactions. For example, Genex, a Yugoslav trading company, uses existing global market information asymmetry to profit from CT deals. Genex maintains offices in major world markets and, hence, has more market knowledge than other firms in the region, particularly the government-owned enterprises in Central and Eastern Europe. Some Genex transactions involve discounts of up to 75%, providing enormous profit opportunities for the firm. However, CT must be used with great care, and unless firms plan CT activities very carefully, costly mistakes can easily occur.

A seemingly convincing argument for engaging in CT is that at least some of the firm's competitors have entered or are willing to negotiate such transactions. Clearly, there are situations where a firm must protect its market by meeting the competition head-on. A case in point is the Japanese success in China, where the U.S. equipment companies lost deals to their rivals because they could not find a market for Chinese products (*The Wall Street Journal*, 1985). Also, some firms with extensive distribution resources may have sufficient internal expertise to bypass at least part of the problems outlined in this article. If an appropriate target market can be identified for CT merchandise, as Carter and Gagne (1988) suggest, the seller can act as a *trading company* and make CT activities a profit center, i.e. internationally market CT merchandise. GE Trading Company and Coca-Cola Trading are two firms whose international CT activities are stand-alone profit centers. To do business in some countries, Coca-Cola must market the CT products it receives globally, e.g. Polish beer in the U.S., and Yugoslavian wine in Japan (*The Wall Street Journal*, 1985). Thus, as in the case of Genex, Coca-Cola uses its market and marketing knowledge to bridge the information gap. In all of these cases, the *trading companies* are acting as *CT channel intermediaries and consultants* to others firms and countries. Strictly speaking, their roles are quite apart from *manufacturers* who profit from market information asymmetry and use their market access to profit from CT, i.e. the presence of trading firms, whether or not they are affiliated with manufacturers, does not add credence to CT activities.

Information and distribution opportunities open to such global marketers as Coca-Cola, however, are uncommon. For most firms, a deliberate acceptance of a CT deal instead of negotiating for monetary transactions can significantly erode the organization's effectiveness and its profitability. In any event, the proportion of CT deals should be kept to a minimum. In general, CT transactions should not exceed 15% of the gross revenues of firms.[16] Nevertheless, the firm's initial objective in entering negotiations, and one that it should work very hard for, must be to transact a monetary deal. That is, the firm must aim for transactions involving no CT, but be open-minded and skillfully consider and negotiate CT deals to preserve its market share and competitive position such that *it meets its financial objectives* as though it were executing a money-based transaction. Still, the firm must always guard itself against the unexpected. In most cases, the negotiating skills of and strategies used by trading organizations in developing and emerging markets are not easily matched by their Western counterparts. A deal may begin as a cash deal, but once prices have been negotiated, either by design or default, the transaction may partly or solely involve CT products (*Business International*, 1980).

Another strong argument for engaging in CT is that of using excess capacity. This, too is not a sufficient reason for engaging in CT and, like all other important corporate decisions, the use of CT because of excess capacity should be policy-driven. If excess capacity is expected to be short-lived, e.g. three months, by definition any market to which this "excess" is sold should be new. If a CT opportunity represents *new business*, is it possible for the firm to lower its price (to CT-deal equivalent level, as shown in Fig. 1) and find *new business* for cash and thus bypass the hurdles and challenges of CT? Even when a discounted cash transaction is not on the horizon, by the time a CT-agreement is reached the firm may no longer have excess capacity. This is also true for cases when the firm has a short term inventory build-up. When excess capacity is expected to last indefinitely, then CT is neither an immediate nor an optimum solution. If the present market(s) is not likely to recover or grow in the long-run, then the firm needs to re-examine its product's strategic position within the firm and consider other possibilities, including joint ventures and direct investment in new markets.

Organization effectiveness is a key consideration in CT. Other than CT departments or specialists "experts" within the firm are generally trained to conduct and profit from conventional deals. Statements made by some CT advocates (e.g. Carter & Gagne, 1988; Elderkin & Norquist, 1987) suggest the development of a whole new way of thinking to gain managerial support to create the understanding that doing business internationally requires using various forms of CT. The difficulties associated with training personnel for CT, the marketing of CT products internally, and the organizational and functional issues raised in this article basically undermine the validity of this position.

Information gathered for this study suggests that relatively small firms do not and *normally should not* engage in CT. This is understandable since uncertainty, time, and the costs associated with CT present unacceptable risks for smaller firms. In addition, CT transactions are generally very large and are beyond the production and financing capabilities of most small firms. A $1 million CT transaction is considered a small one; typical transactions could involve delivery of $150,000 to $300,000 of goods per month for one year, but certain transactions involving consumer goods, namely apparel, can be in the $500,000 range.

Pricing, in particular, is both a sensitive subject from the buyer's perspective and a difficult area from the seller's viewpoint because a supplier's price, and thus margins, will have to vary depending on the cost of disposing of CT merchandise. Concurrently, the firm must come up with a market price and appropriate trade discounts for CT products. A key to success is to stay within the firm's areas of expertise or make certain that its acquisition is not prohibitively expensive.

The ultimate viability of CT is dependent on assessing the *opportunity costs* associated with direct and indirect resources allocated to CT activities. As shown in Fig. 1, profits from CT activities should exceed expected returns from alternative uses of funds and be equal to or greater than profitability achieved though monetary transactions. Alternatives available to the firm include foreign direct investment, expansion in existing or new markets, and development of new products.

NOTES

1. As the Russian market opened up in 1991 and the country rapidly adopted market economy principles, repatriation was no longer an obstacle to trade and, as a result, PepsiCo has sold its U.S. distribution rights for Stolichnaya vodka to Grand Metropolitan and Monsieur Henri to Sazerac Company, a New Orleans based firm.

2. Buy-back refers to the sale of plant, equipment, or technology in exchange for products produced by such transfers. The assumption here is that the seller is very familiar with the products it will eventually receive and can either use the products internally or sell them to others (i.e., seller's own specifications, technology, or brand). Buy-back deals in which the seller receives merchandise that it has no internal need for nor has the expertise to sell externally are subject to the same argument and framework developed in this study. In any event, it is expected that the majority of CT deals do not involve buy-backs. Neale and Shipley (1990) examined CT involvement of British firms and found that 63% participated in counterpurchase whereas 28% of firms were involved in direct exchange (or barter), and only 3% of the firms surveyed were involved in buy-back deals. It is also noteworthy that only 20% of buy-back deals are ever completed (Bussard, 1984a).

3. Switch-traders are intermediaries who sell or transfer CT credits to third parties.

4. There is also evidence that various U.S. Government offices are critical of CT on the basis that it is anti-competitive in nature, it is inefficient, it complicates the tax liability of firms, and it limits the availability of foreign exchange for nations that must repay their foreign debt (*Business Week*, 1980; Cornell, 1983; Czinkota & Ronkainen, 1990; Lange, 1981; McVey, 1984; Suro-Bredie, 1983).

5. The formation of groups of firms that collect and disseminate CT information only among themselves is a further indication of this *modus operandi* (Lecraw, 1989). Most firms retain a similar posture with regard to their product development and product failure news and, from these perspectives, their actions are understandable. On the one hand, firms may perceive loss of competitive advantage by publicizing their CT deals. On the other hand, when losses or less-than-optimal results have been achieved, firms choose to avoid negative publicity.

6. This item was self-reported by respondents in terms of the percentage of countertrade transactions in which they made a profit, broke-even, or lost money. Given the complex nature of CT and the possibility of using a variety of costing methods, these findings are likely to be somewhat subjective in nature and influenced by the profit expectation of firms. For example, a firm can show a profit with greater ease if it uses contribution pricing (i.e. allowing cash deals to pay for the overhead), but since the true cost of engaging in CT transactions is unknown, it may never know its actual profits.

7. OPEC members, China, Mexico, and Russia are just a few of the nations with substantial natural resources. Russia, as a major source of numerous minerals (e.g. bauxite, chromium, lead, manganese, natural gas, oil, platinum, tin, zinc), for example, should be able to raise cash by selling its commodities on the open market.

8. The classical theory can be extended to include other facets of marketing programs, e.g. brand image, delivery, promotion, product design and quality, in addition to or instead of price.

9. The exception is a statement made by Mirus and Yeung (1986) to the effect that aside from net gains, there is also more certainty regarding long-run market access, and hence CT is economically more efficient than money deals (p. 36). This argument is baseless because business practices in countries frequently involved in CT cannot support the assumptions underlying this statement. Indeed, from a marketing perspective, uncertainty regarding brand identity, high and consistent quality, and/or reliable delivery terms should inhibit sellers from engaging in CT deals. Findings by Bussard (1983) regarding these issues support this argument.

10. Although this is the case for the great majority of CT deals, there are some exceptions. Apparel contracts, a common form of CT in Eastern Europe, for example, utilize unused production capacities and frequently require the use of specific fabrics, colors, and designs. This form of CT is analogous to contract manufacturing and should be viewed and treated as such.

CT deals that are inter-linked, i.e. the consummation of the deal depends on sales of the CT products, are still subjected to the reverse marketing system as the market potential, price, and distribution would have to be determined for the merchandise to be received in a CT deal. In situations where inter-linked CT deals are not consummated, the up-front reverse marketing expenses are simply wasted.

11. One exception is the contract manufacturing of products (e.g. apparel) for Western firms using known brands.

12. Certain industrial products including RAM chips, wire and cable, and fasteners may appear more difficult to differentiate. Even for these seemingly homogeneous products, industrial users, and hence suppliers, almost invariably emphasize quality, delivery, service, and other product attributes. The failure rate of RAM chips, for example, varies from one manufacturer to another.

13. In non-routine situations where the seller is contemplating a CT transaction because of excess capacity or excess supply of a product, it is easier to show a profit depending on the price level used by the firm in its computations. Setting a price for a product that faces soft domestic demand and is in an over-supply situation remains a matter of executive judgement.

14. Recipients of such services may find that their management and internal distribution may be too cumbersome. Additionally, certain industries, such as airline and lodging, rely heavily on the business clientele for their livelihood. The exchanging of their particular services must be carefully planned so that it does not interfere with their normal business and cause cannibalization.

15. The Internal Revenue Service has pursued firms for underestimating their revenues as a result of CT deals, in particular barter, for some time (see, for example, *Business Week*, 1980). This is understandable since lower revenue assessment or under-reporting of market values of CT transactions leads to lower profits and, hence, lower tax liabilities. Greater interest and activity in international CT is likely to intensify investigation of such forms of trade by the IRS.

16. Historically, some industries, e.g., aerospace and military hardware, have depended more heavily on CT for securing orders. Though the theoretical underpinnings and the arguments set forth in this article apply equally to all industries, it is clear that firms cannot single-handedly change the patterns of trade in their respective industries overnight.

REFERENCES

Aaby, N. E., & Slater, S. F. (1989). Management influences on export performance: A review of the empirical literature 1978–1988. *International Marketing Review, 6*(4), 41–57.
Bertrand, K. (1986). Creative deal-making pays off for countertrade unit. *Business Marketing* (August), 24.
Business International (1980). Selling to eastern Europe? Keep in mind the tricks of the (counter) trade. November 28.
Business Week (1980). Using barter as a way of doing business (August 4), 57.
Bussard, W. A. (1983). *A view of countertrade*. The National Foreign Trade Council Foundation, New York, December 15.
Bussard, W. A. (1984a). Countertrade: A view from U.S. industry. *Countertrade and Barter Quarterly* (May), 53–55.
Bussard, W. A. (1984b). U.S. traders must coalesce on exports. *American Banker* (September 21), 31.
Carter, J. R., & Gagne, J. (1988). The dos and don'ts of international countertrade. *Sloan Management Review, 29*(Spring), 31–37.
Claycamp, H. J., & Massy, W. S. (1968). A theory of market segmentation. *Journal of Marketing Research, 5*(November), 388–394.
Cohen, S. S., & Zysman, J. (1986). Countertrade, offsets, barter, and buybacks. *California Management Review, 28*(2), 41–56.
Cornell, R. A. (1983). Deputy Assistant Secretary, U.S. Department of the Treasury, testimony before the U.S. Senate Subcommittee on Preparedness of the Committee on Armed Services, 98th Congress, 1st session, November 18.
Czinkota, M. R., & Ronkainen, I. A. (1990). *International Marketing* (pp. 700–721). Chicago: Dryden Press.
Damitio, J. W., Schmidgall, R. S., & Kintzele, P. (1995). Bartering activities of fortune 500 companies. *The National Public Accountant, 40*(3), 21–24.
Davis, R. (2002). A deal with strings attached. *Financial Times, 10*(July 18).
The Economist (1985). Countertrade comes out of the closet (December 20), 86.
Elderkin, K. W., & Norquist, W. E. (1987). *Creative countertrade*. Cambridge, MA: Ballinger Press.
Financial Times (1984). Countertrade wins a stamp of respectability (October 25), 5.
James, M. (1986). Saudi Arabia pays for British Aircraft with barrels of oil. *Euromoney* (August), 105.
Kassaye, W. W. (1985). Countertrade prospects and dilemma for small businesses. *American Journal of Small Business, 9*(Winter), 17–24.
Lange, J. D., Jr. (1981). Director, Office of Trade Finance, U.S. Department of the Treasury, Testimony before the House of Representatives, Economic Stabilization Subcommittee, Committee on Banking, Finance, and Urban Affairs, 97th Congress, 1st Session, September 24.
Lecraw, D. J. (1987). Countertrade as a form of international cooperative arrangement. In: J. Farok & P. Lorange (Eds), *Cooperative Strategies in International Business*. Lexington, MA: Lexington Books, D. C. Heath & Co.

Lecraw, D. J. (1989). The management of countertrade: Factors influencing success. *Journal of International Business Studies* (Spring), 41–59.

Lo, H. Y. (1995). Risk management in trade with central European Countries. *Management International Review*, *35*(Special Issue), 123–132.

McVey, T. B. (1984). Countertrade: Commercial practices, legal issues, and policy dilemmas. *Law and Policy in International Business* (January), 57.

de Miramon, J. (1982). Countertrade: A modern form of barter. *OECD Observer* (January), 12.

Mirus, R., & Yeung, B. (1986). Economic incentives for countertrade. *Journal of International Business Studies* (Fall), 27–39.

Neale, C. W., & Shipley, D. D. (1990). Empirical insights into British countertrade with Eastern Bloc countries. *International Marketing Review*, *7*(1), 15–31.

The New York Times (1990a). Pepsi will be bartered for ships and vodka in deal with Soviets (April 9), 1.

The New York Times (1990b). IBM signs pact with Soviets, June 2.

Rabino, S., & Shah, K. (1987). Countertrade and penetration of LDC markets. *Columbia Journal of World Business* (Winter), 31–37.

Rugman, A. M., Lecraw, D. J., & Booth, L. D. (1986). *International Business: Firm and Environment.* NY: McGraw-Hill.

Schaffer, M. (1990). Countertrade as an export strategy. *The Journal of Business Strategy*, *11*(3) (May–June), 33–38.

Shipley, D. D., & Neale, C. W. (1987). Industrial barter and countertrade. *Industrial Marketing Management*, *16*(1) (February), 1–9.

Suro-Bredie, C. (1983). Director of South-East Asian Affairs, U.S. Trade Representative, testimony before the House of Representatives, Subcommittee on Sea-Power and Strategic and Critical Materials, Committee on Armed Services, 98th Congress, 1st Session, October 19.

U.S. Export Weekly (1982). GATT director dunkel criticizes trend toward unilateral trade law interpretations (July 20), 557.

The Wall Street Journal (1985). Japanese dominate the Chinese market with savvy trading (November 8), 1.

MNC CONTROL OVER FOREIGN MARKET VENTURES: DO HOST GOVERNMENTS STILL PLAY A MAJOR ROLE?

Shaoming Zou, Charles R. Taylor and Er (Eric) Fang

ABSTRACT

While it is widely acknowledged that host governments play some role in framing the governance structure that is available to multinational corporations, some argue that in recent years the influence of host governments on MNCs in terms of the level of ownership and control over their foreign ventures has diminished. The authors examine the degree of MNC's control in foreign investment by presenting and testing a model of government influences on MNC's control over its foreign market venture. Based on a survey of U.S. MNCs, the authors find that host government preference does influence MNC's ownership control over its foreign market venture, which in turn influences its management control over the venture.

INTRODUCTION

Recent times have seen an increasingly linked global economy. With the shift toward more market-oriented economies in Russia, China, Latin America, and Eastern Europe along with the growth of economies in other parts of the world, opportunities for partnerships and/or foreign investment have increased. Many

Reviving Traditions in Research on International Market Entry
Advances in International Marketing, Volume 14, 35–47
© 2003 Published by Elsevier Science Ltd.
ISSN: 1474-7979/doi:10.1016/S1474-7979(03)14003-3

multinational corporations (MNCs) have taken advantage of such opportunities by expanding into more and more foreign markets. A large volume of research has examined the foreign market entry strategies of MNCs. While it is widely acknowledged that host governments play some role in framing the governance structure that is available to multinational corporations, some argue that in recent years the influence of host governments on MNCs in terms of the level of ownership and control over their foreign ventures has diminished due to forces such as globalization along with increased competition for foreign investments (e.g. Jenkins, 1986; Makhija, 1993). An interesting research question is, thus, "Do host governments still play a major role in shaping MNCs' control in their foreign ventures?"

The purpose of this paper is to examine the extent to which host governments and their policies still influence MNCs' equity stake and perceived level of management control. In order to examine these relationships, a model is proposed and tested based on the results of a large-scale survey of U.S. MNC executives.

The remainder of this paper will begin by examining the role of control in foreign investment. This is followed by the introduction of a model of government influences on MNC's control over its foreign market venture. Hypotheses pertaining to the relationship between the factors in the model will be developed and discussed. Next, our methodology will be described in detail. This is followed by a discussion of results and implications. Limitations are then discussed and conclusions drawn.

CONCEPTUAL FRAMEWORK

The Role of Level of Control

The level of managerial control a firm has over a foreign venture can clearly influence its success in terms of both profitability and market share (Pan, Li & Tse, 1999). Thus, prior theories of foreign direct investment have emphasized the central role of control in choosing a governance structure (Davis, Desai & Francis, 2000). High levels of equity control are important when a firm has proprietary assets or production processes since it allows a firm to worry less about the protection of those assets (Anand & Delios, 1997; Buckley & Casson, 1976; Caves, 1982). Additionally, high levels of control are associated with less potential for conflicting goals among partners getting in the way of the venture's management and performance (Pan, Li & Tse 1999).

The advantages afforded by a high degree of control do not mean that MNCs will always have a strong preference for full ownership or other high equity arrangements. If an investing company needs a partner to provide complementary assets or skills that it does not possess, it may choose to enter a low control arrangement (Hennart & Larimo, 1998).

Clearly, host governments will seldom stand in the way when a MNC would like to partner with a local firm. Because of a desire to keep at least some equity and decision-making power within the country, the natural tendency in many countries has historically been to place restrictions on levels of equity a firm can obtain, or at least to negotiate on this issue (Jenkins, 1986). With significant local participation, the host country hopes to better learn from MNCs and avoid the impression of letting MNCs exploit local consumers and businesses. Our focus is examining the extent to which host governments still affect the level of control attained by MNCs in foreign investments.

The Model and Research Hypotheses

The host government's role is at the heart of the bargaining power (BP) theory of foreign investment (e.g. Brouthers & Bamossy, 1997; Fagre & Wells, 1982; LeCraw, 1984; Vachiani, 1995). Traditionally, BP theory has looked at the governance structure chosen by the firm as being the result of negotiations between the firm as the host government. As such, factors including the government's stake in attracting an investment, along with its preferences and specific regulations have been thought to play a major role in the form of foreign investment made in a country. Within a bargaining power framework, it can be posited that the level of control a firm achieves is heavily influenced by the host government's policies. A conceptual model of this influence and its impact on both entry mode and control is shown in Fig. 1.

The model predicts that the equity control of a MNC over its foreign market entry is a function of both the stake of the host government in attracting the investment and the degree to which the government would prefer the MNC enter into a mode of entry that involves less MNC control. The MNC's equity control in its entry mode, in turn, is hypothesized to interact with specific government limitations in influencing the MNC's perceived level of management control over strategy and operations over its foreign venture. Individual components of the model are discussed below in conjunction with hypothesis development.

Control of Foreign Ventures

The primary dependent variables in the model are MNC's management control and equity control. As conceptualized in this study, management control is a composite of the firm's control over both strategy and operations of its foreign market venture.

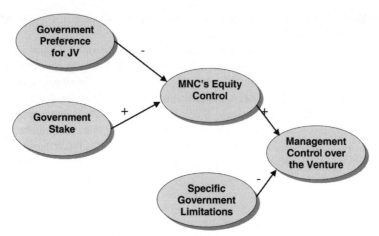

Fig. 1. A Model of Host Government Influence on MNC's Control.

In terms of strategy, control refers to the degree to which the MNC has authority over decisions that affect the firm's long-term direction and strategic focus. In contrast, operational control refers to the degree to which the firm oversees the day to day operations of the business.

MNC's equity control is defined as the percentage of MNC's equity position in its foreign market venture. A MNC may take a zero equity position by choosing franchising or licensing mode to enter the foreign market. It may also take a minority or a majority equity position in a joint venture with local firms. Finally, it may assume 100% control by establishing a wholly-owned subsidiary in the foreign market. Variables posited to impact MNC control are discussed below.

Stake of the Host Government

The degree to which the host government desires to attract the MNC's investment has been found to play a role in the entry mode chosen by the firm (Brouthers & Bamossy, 1997; LeCraw, 1984). In general, when the host government has a high stake in attracting the investment, the MNC has a greater possibility of negotiating for a high control entry mode, such as full ownership or a majority controlled joint venture (Gomes-Casseres, 1990). The host country may have a high stake when it views the investment as having the potential to increase employment or make a positive contribution to the local economy. Thus:

H1. When the host government has a high stake in attracting an investment, the MNC is more likely to enter the foreign market with a high equity control entry mode (e.g. full ownership or a majority joint venture).

Host Government Preference for a Joint Venture

Whether based on specific laws or negotiating policies, the host government's preference for a certain ownership type has been hypothesized to play a major role in the structure of foreign investments (Davidson & McFeteridge, 1985; Gomes-Casseres, 1990). For example, if the host government expects significant local participation in ventures in the country or simply has a political preference for joint ventures, it is more likely that a firm will not be able to achieve a majority equity position in the venture. Similarly, if the host government encourages the investor to enter a joint venture through incentives because of a preference for minority ownership by MNCs, it is less likely that investors will achieve majority ownership. Thus:

H2. When the host government preference for a joint venture is high, the MNC is less likely to enter the foreign market with a high equity control entry mode (e.g. full ownership or a majority joint venture).

MNC's Equity Control

A MNC may adopt a variety of ownership structures for its new venture into a foreign market. Major methods of entry include exporting, licensing and franchising, joint ventures, and full ownership of the venture (Root, 1994). Since exporting is a relatively low risk proposition that requires less investment in a foreign market, such cases are not included in our analysis (see also Pan, Li & Tse, 1999). For the purposes of this study, the key distinction is whether the firm has minority ownership (licensing/franchising or a minority joint ventures) vs. having majority ownership (majority joint venture or full ownership). In addition to asking respondents about the entry mode of a recent venture, in this study we also inquired about the degree of management control over strategic decisions and daily operations of the firm. Prior research has clearly suggested that majority joint ventures and full ownership are associated with higher levels of management control over both strategy and operations. Thus:

H3. A MNC with a high degree of equity control in its foreign venture is more likely to gain a high degree of management control over the strategy and operations of its foreign venture.

Specific Government Limitations on the Firm's Operations

Government laws and policies pertaining to foreign-owned ventures are also likely to have an impact on the level of control a firm realizes over its operations. If firms are inhibited by laws such as exchange controls, profit repatriation limits, or other restrictive regulations, they are less likely to have high levels of management control over their ventures' strategy and operations. Exchange controls, which refer to laws on the free use of foreign exchange are sometimes imposed by countries with an unfavorable balance of trade (Davidson & McFeteridge, 1985). Similarly, profit repatriation limits, which governments may impose to limit the amount of income that can leave the country, tend to reduce the firm's level of management control. In general, any limitation on the firm's options compared to what they face at home or in other markets may reduce the level of control they perceive over the venture. Thus:

H4. A MNC operating in a country characterized by extensive specific government limitations on foreign ventures is less likely to gain a high level of management control over the venture.

METHODOLOGY

Sampling Frame

Data used for this study was drawn from a survey of U.S. manufacturing MNCs. Manufacturing industries were selected as the population for two reasons. First, few known studies have collected primary data on the entry strategies of U.S. manufacturing firms. Second, prior literature suggests that there are differences in considerations involved in entry mode choice between service industries and manufacturing industries (Agarwal & Ramaswami, 1992; Erramilli & Rao, 1993).

The sampling frame of strategic business units (SBUs) was identified using Dun and Bradstreet's American Corporate Families. These sources listed the firm's annual sales, number of employees, and key contact persons. Only firms with at least 100 employees and $20 million in annual sales were included. These criteria were considered necessary to enhance the relative homogeneity of the sample, and were consistent with the focus of the research, namely firms of sufficient size to have a range of possibilities in terms of entry mode arrangements and management control.

Questionnaire and Measures

A structured survey questionnaire was developed using a multi-stage process. First, prior literature was reviewed to identify measures relevant to the study. Second, a list of items that were potentially useful in measuring the factors in the model was developed. These items were then expanded into Likert-type statements answered on a five-point scale ranging from "strongly agree" to "strongly disagree."

The third stage was to pretest the questionnaire via personal interviews with three executives responsible for international market ventures and with academicians familiar with research on foreign direct investment. Based on feedback from these interviews, some items were dropped and others were modified. Prior to finalizing the questionnaire, the survey was administered to several business executives in order to evaluate the validity of the revised items and the amount of time it took to complete the survey. After incorporating feedback from these additional pretests, the questionnaire was finalized. The specific items used in this study are listed in Table 1.

Data Collection

Data collection involved several phases. In the initial phase, a personalized cover letter, a questionnaire, and a postage-paid business reply envelope were sent to the CEO/President or the VP of International Operations of each of the SBUs in the sampling frame. The cover letter explained the importance of participation in the study, described the time and effort needed to complete the questionnaire, assured confidentiality, and promised a summary report of the study's findings upon request. Five weeks after the initial mailing, an additional mailing, which included a replacement copy of the questionnaire was sent out to those SBUs that had not responded in the first mailing.

Eventually, 165 usable responses were obtained from the survey. After eliminating those that were not deliverable, an effective response rate of 18.0% was achieved. Potential non-response bias was assessed by comparing the responding SBUs with non-responding SBUs in terms of annual sales and number of full-time employees, the only comparative data available for both responding and non-responding groups. No significant differences were found in terms of average annual sales and average number of employees.

Measures

Management control over the venture, the primary dependent measure in the study, was measured by two questions. The first question asked, "What level of control does your company have over the strategic decisions of your recent venture into this foreign market." The second was essentially the same, except that it asked about the level of control over daily operations instead of strategic decisions. Both

Table 1. CFA Measurement Model.

Items	Standardized Loadings	t-Value
Government preference		
1. This foreign governmnet expects significant local participation in the management of our venture.	0.65	6.28
2. This foreign government offers important incentives for investing in a joint venture, as opposed to a wholly-owned subsidiary.	0.52	4.82
3. The host government prefers a joint venture to a wholly-owned subsidiary.	0.78	7.74
Specific government limitations		
1. There is extensive government control over foreign exchange in this foreign country.	0.78	7.15
2. This foreign government has significant restrictions on our ability to repatriate the profits made from this venture.	0.63	5.78
3. The foreign government imposes many restrictions on our access to the local market.	0.54	4.85
Government stake		
1. Our investment in this foreign market is extremely important to the host country.	0.52	3.07
2. To the host country, the cost of not winning our investment there is very high.	0.56	4.48
Management control over the venture		
1. What level of control does your company have over the strategic decisions of your recent venture into this foreign market? (no control at all . . . total control)	0.77	6.91
2. What level of control does your company have over the daily operations of your recent venture into this foreign market? (no control at all . . . total control)	0.73	6.65
MNC's equity control		
What kind of arrangement did your business unit use for your recent entry into this foreign country? Licensing/franchising 1 Minority joint venture 2 Majority joint venture 3 Wholly-wholly subsidiary 4	0.93	

Fit Indices: Chi-Square (df $= 36$): 43.819, $p > 0.10$; GFI: 0.92; CFI: 0.96; NFI: 0.84, and RMSR: 0.08.

questions used five-point semantic differential scales with endpoints of "no control at all," and "total control."

To measure *government preference for a joint venture*, three questions using the aforementioned five-point Likert scales were used. These were: (1) "This foreign government expects significant local participation in the management of our venture," (2) "The foreign government offers important incentives for investing in a joint venture as opposed to a wholly-owned subsidiary," and (3) "The host government prefers a joint venture to a wholly-owned subsidiary."

The *government's stake* in attracting the investment was measured by two Likert-type items. These were: (1) "Our investment in this market is extremely important to the host country," and (2) "To the host country, the cost of not winning our investment there is very high."

The *specific government limitations* construct was measured via three Likert items. These were: (1) "There is extensive government control over foreign exchange in this foreign country," (2) "The foreign government has significant restrictions on our ability to repatriate the profits made from this venture," and (3) "The foreign government imposes many restrictions on our access to the market."

MNC's equity control in its foreign venture was measured by one item. Specifically, respondents were asked to indicate whether their foreign venture was a licensing agreement or a franchising arrangement (0% equity), a minority joint venture ($\leq$50% equity), a majority joint venture (>50% but <100% equity), or a wholly-owned subsidiary (100% equity). A four-point scale ranged from 1 to 4 was used to represent their answers in among these categories.

Analytical Approach

A two-stage approach is taken to analyze the data and test the proposed model. In the first stage, a confirmatory factor analysis measurement model is assessed using EQS. Once the measurement model fits the data, the path model is then fitted by the ML (maximum likelihood) criterion in EQS in the second stage. According to Anderson and Gerbing (1988), the two-stage approach to model fitting has two main advantages. First, it is less demanding on the sample size due to the reduced model at each stage. Second, the potential confounding effect between the structural model and the measurement model can be avoided.

Measurement Assessment

Confirmatory factor analysis (CFA) was used to estimate the measurement model that composed of five latent factors. Following Gerbing and Anderson (1988), we estimated a measurement model in which each item was restricted to load on a priori specified factor, and the factors themselves were permitted to be correlated.

We obtained maximum likelihood estimates of the measurement model (see Table 1) using EQS. The overall chi-square statistic for the model was significant (χ^2(df = 35) = 56.938, $p < 0.05$), as might be expected given the size of our sample (Bagozzi & Yi, 1988). However, the comparative fit index (0.96); Bentler and Bonett's (1980) normed fit index (0.91); the goodness fit index (0.95) and the root mean square residual (0.07) all pointed to evidence of good model fit. Moreover, all factor loadings were positive and significant at 0.01 level. The measurement model thus provides satisfactory evidence of the internal consistency of the factors. The coefficient alpha for each scale also provides satisfactory evidence of reliability.

Next, we estimated a set of additional models in which the correlation between each pair of factors was restricted to unity. We compared the fit of the restricted models with that of the unrestricted models by chi-square difference test. The various chi-square difference tests were all significant and provided evidence of discriminant validity (Bagozzi, Yi & Phillips, 1991).

Test of the Hypotheses

Path analysis was used to assess the hypothesized model. Data were analyzed using EQS (Bentler, 1995). Path analysis makes it possible to simultaneously test all the hypothesized relationships of the focal constructs and the fit of the proposed model to the data. We mean-centered the items for the constructs to obtain factor scores for path analysis.

The results of the path analysis are presented in Fig. 2. As can be seen, the path model demonstrated an acceptable fit to the data (χ^2 = (df = 3) = 2.269, $p > 0.05$, CFI = 1.00, NFI = 0.97, GFI = 0.99, AGFI = 0.95, RMSR = 0.03). Consequently, the estimates of the path coefficients were considered to adequately represent the relationships among the factors and were used to test the research hypotheses.

Specifically, H1 predicts that host government stake is negatively related to firm's equity control in its foreign market entry mode. This hypothesis is not supported because the path coefficient is not significant ($b = 0.07$, $p > 0.05$). Based on the estimate of the path coefficient, host government preference is found to relate negatively to firm's equity control in its foreign market entry mode ($b = -0.46$, $p < 0.01$). Thus, H2 is supported by the results. Consistent with H3, firm's equity control is positively related to firm's management control over its

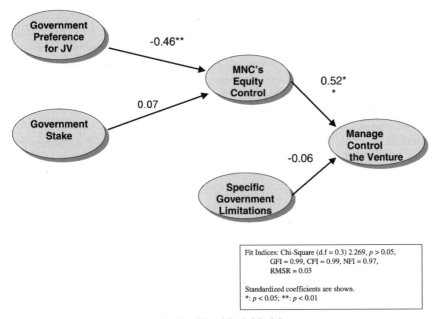

Fit Indices: Chi-Square (d.f = 0.3) 2.269, $p > 0.05$,
GFI = 0.99, CFI = 0.99, NFI = 0.97,
RMSR = 0.03

Standardized coefficients are shown.
*: $p < 0.05$; **: $p < 0.01$

Fig. 2.   Fitted Path Model.

foreign subsidiaries ($b = 0.52$, $p < 0.01$). Finally, it was hypothesized in H4 that host government restrictions are negatively related to company's management control over the foreign market venture. This prediction is not supported by the results because the coefficient of the relationship is not significant ($b = -0.06$, $p > 0.05$). Overall, two of the four hypotheses related to the model are supported by the results.

DISCUSSION AND CONCLUSIONS

While the findings do not provide support for all of the relationships in the proposed model, they are nevertheless interesting. Perhaps most important, the significant negative relationship between government preference for a joint venture and the MNCs equity control (H2) suggests that host government preference is still a very relevant factor in the governance structure obtained by the investing firm. The fact that this finding is significant implies that host governments who strongly prefer that the MNC enter through a low control governance structure, expect local participation, and offer incentives to do so, tend to get their wish. Interestingly, the fact that the government's stake in attracting the investment was not found to have a significant impact on MNC equity control (H1), suggests that government preference for a joint venture operates at least somewhat independently of the stake the government has in attracting the investment. Thus, the government's preference, which may be based on a desire for an existing regime to strengthen the economy with local involvement, or on other political factors appears to be very important.

The findings of this study indicate that specific government limitations such as exchange controls, profit repatriation limits, and restrictions on market access have relatively little impact on firms' perceptions of its strategic and operational control. In a way, this makes sense, as such limitations, while placing a specific limit (such as on foreign exchange) on the firm may not be perceived as having a widespread impact on how they do business. Firms may be especially prone to not believing that such limitation reduce control since they know about the constraints in advance.

A key implication of the relationship between MNC's equity control and management control over the venture (H3) is that it indicates firms view full ownership as offering more control than majority joint ventures, which in turn offer more control than minority joint ventures and other arrangements.

Taken collectively, these findings suggest at least some support for studying foreign market entry from a bargaining power perspective. While very specific restrictions may not have much impact on management perceived level of control, the government's preference often does. Thus, for MNCs, the host government's preferences still often play a significant role in management's equity, strategic, and operational control over the venture. Hence, even in this era of increased competition for investments and a more linked global economy, the host government's preferences still matter and theoreticians are well advised to weigh this factor in models of foreign market entry.

REFERENCES

Agarwal, S., & Ramaswami, S. N. (1992). Choice of foreign market entry mode: Impact of ownership, location, and internalization factors. *Journal of International Business Studies, 23*(1), 1–27.

Anand, J., & Delios, A. (1997). Location specificity and the transferability of downstream assets to foreign subsidiaries. *Journal of International Business Studies, 28,* 579–603.

Anderson, J. C., & Gerbing, D. W. (1988). Structural equations modeling in practice: A review and recommended two-step approach. *Psychological Bulletin, 103*(3), 411–423.

Bentler, P. M. (1995). *EQS structural equations program manual.* Los Angeles, CA: Multivariate Software.

Brouthers, K. D., & Bamossy, G. J. (1997). The role of key stakeholders in international joint venture negotiations: Case studies from Eastern Europe. *Journal of International Business Studies, 28,* 85–308.

Buckley, P. J., & Casson, M. C. (1976). *The future of the multinational enterprise.* London: Holmes and Meier.

Caves, R. E. (1982). *Multinational enterprise and economic analysis.* Cambridge: Cambridge University Press.

Davidson, W. H., & McFeteridge, D. G. (1985). Key characteristics in the choice of international technology transfer mode. *Journal of International Business Studies, 16*(Summer), 5–22.

Davis, P. S., Desai, A. B., & Francis, J. D. (2000). Mode of international entry: An isomorphic perspective. *Journal of International Business Studies, 31*(2), 239–258.

Erramilli, M. K., & Rao, C. P. (1993). Service firms' international entry mode choice: A modified transaction cost analysis approach. *Journal of Marketing, 57*(July), 19–38.

Fagre, N., & Wells, L. T. (1982). Bargaining power of multinationals and host governments. *Journal of International Business Studies, 13,* 9–23.

Gerbing, D. W., & Anderson, J. C. (1988). An updated paradigm for scale development incorporating unidimensionality and its assessment. *Journal of Marketing Research, 25*(May), 186–192.

Gomes-Casseres, B. (1990). Firm ownership preferences and host government restrictions: An integrated approach. *Journal of International Business Studies, 21,* 1–21.

Hennart, J. F., & Larimo, J. (1998). The impact of culture on the strategy of multinational enterprises: Does national origin affect ownership decisions. *Journal of International Business Studies, 29*(3), 515–538.

Jenkins, B. (1986). Re-examining the 'obsolescing bargain': A study of Canada's National Energy Program. *International Organization, 40,* 139–165.

LeCraw, D. J. (1984). Bargaining power, ownership and profitability of transnational corporations in developing countries. *Journal of International Business Studies, 15,* 27–42.

Makhija, M. V. (1993). Government intervention in the Venezualan Petroleum Industry: An empirical investigation of political risk. *Journal of International Business Studies, 23,* 531–555.

Pan, Y., Li, S., & Tse, D. K. (1999). The impact of order and mode of market entry on profitability and market share. *Journal of International Business Studies, 30,* 81–104.

Root, F. R. (1994). *Entry strategies for international markets.* Washington, DC: Lexington Books.

Vachiani, S. (1995). Enhancing the obsolescing bargain theory: A longitudinal study of the foreign ownership of U.S. and European multinationals. *Journal of International Business Studies, 26,* 159–180.

CHANNEL INTEGRATION DECISIONS IN NEW PRODUCT GLOBAL COMPETITION: A CONCEPTUAL FRAMEWORK AND EMPIRICAL EXAMINATION

Tiger Li and Zhan G. Li

ABSTRACT

Although research on channel integration has evolved into a major stream in literature in international marketing, channel integration in new product export remains unexamined. Drawing on transaction cost analysis, organizational capability, and marketing control perspectives, the authors develop a conceptual model of channel integration in new product export. They further test the model using data collected from the computer software industry. The findings indicate that both channel integration and new product competitive advantage exert positive impacts on product market performance in foreign markets. The results regarding asset specificity, country risk, and firm size offer interesting insights about the linkage between these antecedents and channel integration.

Reviving Traditions in Research on International Market Entry
Advances in International Marketing, Volume 14, 49–75
© 2003 Published by Elsevier Science Ltd.
ISSN: 1474-7979/doi:10.1016/S1474-7979(03)14004-5

1. INTRODUCTION

The degree of channel integration is an important issue in new product export and international marketing. At the upper end of the integration, a firm can establish a wholly-owned subsidiary in a foreign market and perform all the marketing functions itself in new product distribution. At the lower end, a firm can contract an independent distributor and consign all the tasks of product introduction. In between, a firm may choose intermediary options such as forming an equity alliance with a foreign partner. These choices have a significant impact on product market performance because each level of integration offers a firm a different degree of control and capability in new product introduction in a foreign market.

This research centers on the issue of channel integration in new product export. Over the last decade, channel integration has become a major theme in a stream of literature in international marketing management. Based on a transaction-cost analysis, Klein, Frazier and Roth (1990) develop a conceptual framework to explain channel integration choices of firms in international markets. Erramilli and Rao (1993) use a modified transaction-cost model to predict levels of international entry choices in service industries. Moreover, Kim and Hwang (1992) examine transaction-specific, organizational capability, and strategic factors that influence channel integration in foreign countries. Recently, Aulakh and Kotabe (1997) extend previous studies and address the performance implications of channel integration.

While these studies have enriched our understanding of channel integration, several issues remain unaddressed. First, previous investigations of channel integration focused exclusively on mature products (see Agarwal & Ramaswami, 1992; Anderson & Gatignon, 1986; Aulakh & Kotabe, 1997; Erramilli & Rao, 1993; Kim & Hwang, 1992 for reviews on this literature). As a result, entry mode choice for new product export is not yet examined. Second, among prior studies, few explored the impact of channel integration on product market performance. Although Aulakh and Kotabe (1997) present an exception, their study was designed to assess overall channel performance without regard to effects on new product performance. Third, previous studies (Aulakh & Kotabe, 1997; Erramilli & Rao, 1993; Kim & Hwang, 1992) placed an emphasis on the effect of asset specificity on channel integration. However, their asset specificity was operationalized for investment in service industries or general business and is not readily applicable to investment in new product development. Fourth, product competitive advantage is assumed to play a critical role in export channel performance (Cavusgil & Kirpalani, 1993). Recently, based on an organizational capability perspective, Madhok (1997) calls for an examination of organizational competitiveness in channel distribution. Yet, the impact of firms' product competitive advantage on channel performance remains undocumented.

We address these issues through developing a model of channel integration in new product export. We intend to achieve three objectives with the model: (1) investigating channel choices in new product distribution in foreign markets; (2) assessing the influence of asset specificity and organizational capability factors on channel integration; and (3) examining the impact of channel integration and new product competitive advantage on product market performance.

We believe this study contributes to the literature in international marketing in several ways. First, it attempts to empirically test the impact of transaction-specific and organizational capability factors on channel choices within the context of new product introduction in foreign markets. This is an important goal in view of previous studies on the relationships between factors of transaction cost and channel integration. Prior research advanced the literature by focusing on the effect of transaction-specific factors on the distribution of service products (Erramilli & Rao, 1993) and manufacturing goods in mature industries (Aulakh & Kotabe, 1997; Klein, Frazier & Roth, 1990). Centering on the market entry of innovative products from a high-tech industry, this study represents a contribution to this research stream. Second, this study begins to fill a gap in research on new product performance in export markets. In recent years, the escalation of R&D cost and intensified domestic competition in the U.S. highlight the importance of new product performance in export markets. However, research on the issue is meager. The few existing studies examined either the impact of new product attributes on performance (Cavusgil & Zou, 1994) or the relationship between domestic sales and export performance (Atuahene-Gima, 1995). Focusing on the effect of channel integration on new product performance, this research offers new insights into the performance issue. Third, this study contributes to the understanding of channel integration by explicitly examining its effect on product performance. This is significant since the direct effect of channel integration on market performance is undocumented in the extant channel literature.

We proceed by reviewing three perspectives in export channel integration and product market performance. Collectively, these perspectives provide a conceptual framework for this study. Next, a model of channel integration in new product export is proposed and research hypotheses are developed. Then, we describe the methods used for data collection and model testing. Finally, we discuss implications and future research directions.

2. CONCEPTUAL FRAMEWORK

Over the last decade, channel integration is a central issue in research on product export distribution. Among the contemporary views, transaction cost analysis and organizational capability perspective are prominent offering complementary explanations. A third perspective, rooted in marketing control literature, interprets relationships between channel integration and market performance.

2.1. Transaction Cost Analysis

Under what circumstances should a firm assume distribution functions internally instead of relying on outside intermediaries? Transaction cost analysis (Williamson, 1975, 1985) provides an explanation. The basic premise is that the firm internalizes channel activities when it is able to perform at lower cost and relies on the market for activities in which intermediaries have an advantage (Klein, Frazier & Roth, 1990). The extent to which activities are internalized, and thus control achieved, reflects the transaction costs incurred. Transaction cost analysis is based on assumptions of bounded rationality and self-interest of parties involved in the manufacturer-distributor relationships. Because of vested interests, participants in a channel exchange have a tendency to adjust their behavior opportunistically according to perceived transaction cost (Anderson & Gatignon, 1986). When the cost of participating in an exchange is perceived to be high, the firm will achieve greater efficiency by increasing the level of control over channel activities.

In export markets, the two major factors that determine transaction costs are transaction-specific assets and uncertainty surrounding the transactions (Aulakh & Kotabe, 1997; Erramilli & Rao, 1993; Klein, Frazier & Roth, 1990). Transaction-specific assets refer to non-redeployable physical and human investments that are specialized and unique to a task (Erramilli & Rao, 1993). For example, introduction of a new product requires investment in the development of specialized know-how and technology. Because such assets are specific to the firm, the transaction associated with the assets may not be fairly assessed in the market. Due to opportunistic behavior of intermediaries, a discrepancy in transaction evaluation often occurs between the firm and intermediaries. Under these circumstances, the firm tends to resort to "stringent negotiation and supervision of contractual relationships, thereby greatly increasing the transaction costs associated with low-control modes" (Erramilli & Rao, 1993, p. 21). When this happens, the firm can reduce its transaction costs by establishing subsidiaries to internalize middlemen's functions.

Uncertainty is another major factor. As Williamson (1975, 1985) observes, that external uncertainty is inhibitory to optimal contracting. Recently, Aulakh and Kotabe (1997, p. 151) comment that "when faced with external uncertainty, firms are better off internalizing the transaction by vertically integrating to allow the absorption of uncertainty through specialization of decision making within the firm." However, this view is contended by Lawrence and Lorsch (1967) who consider looser structures, such as those less vertically integrated systems, are more effective in coping with external uncertainty. Subsequent studies (Agarwal & Ramaswami, 1992; Aulakh & Kotabe, 1997; Kim & Hwang, 1992) suggest that the selection of low control mode is attributable to the country risk associated with uncertainty. Firms often choose intermediaries to avoid political instability and economic fluctuations.

2.2. Organizational Capability Perspective

Organizational capability perspective offers a complementary explanation of channel integration. According to the perspective, "the capabilities of firms influence their ability and willingness to invest resources required to make forward and backward integration decisions" (Aulakh & Kotabe, 1997, p. 148). Because firms are limited in their structural and financial capabilities, the scope of their operations in foreign markets is constrained. Channel integration, as a major aspect of foreign operations, is vulnerable to capability constraint. While large firms with access to resources are able to establish subsidiaries, small firms with limited asset are often compelled to make selections at the lower end of channel integration (Agarwal & Ramaswami, 1992). Organizational capability perspective is distinctive in that it is mainly concerned with the impact of organizational resource management on integration decisions, whereas transaction cost analysis centers on transaction characteristics and minimization of the sum of transactions. More recently, Madhok (1997) considers the capability perspective a practical approach more in tune with market context. To guide empirical investigation, several researchers (Aulakh & Kotabe, 1997; Erramilli & Rao, 1993) identify firm size the most salient factor that captures organizational capability.

Furthermore, in his analysis of the capabilities of market-driven organizations, Day (1994) views product competitive advantage a specific market capability of an organization. In a stream of literature in new product development (Cooper, 1992; Griffin & Hauser, 1993; Song & Parry, 1997), this market capability is recognized as a contributing factor to product market performance. Following prior research, we consider product competitive advantage a firm's market capability that will have a direct impact on new product export performance. This is in line with

Madhok (1997) who places an emphasis on investigating the effectiveness of organizational capabilities in enhancing channel performance.

2.3. Marketing Control

Marketing control theorists (Bello & Gilliland, 1997; Jaworski, 1988) view channel integration a major control mechanism that firms can use to achieve market performance goals. In export marketing, vertical integration allows export manufacturers to have jurisdiction over marketing activities and decisions that are vital to market performance. For example, Douglas and Craig (1989) suggest that the ability to control and conduct customer interaction activities in a foreign country has a direct impact on product market acceptance. Cavusgil (1988) identifies the ability to implement pricing policies an important factor to product market success because a foreign manufacturer's market share and sales are directly related to how it responds to local competitors' pricing practice. Further, jurisdiction over retail arrangement allows a firm to efficiently manage and coordinate its logistics operations with local retailers. In contrast, low control modes in channel distribution may impede a manufacturer's market performance. When firms choose low control by exporting through international intermediaries, such as foreign-based distributors, they shift marketing responsibility to their overseas partners as they spin off functions. "Because key functions are delegated, manufacturers find it difficult to coordinate foreign marketing for their products and are vulnerable to low export performance" (Bello & Gilliland, 1997, p. 22).

2.4. Summary

A synthesis of the three perspectives leads to the following propositions: (1) the degree of channel integration in new product export is influenced by both transaction cost and organization capability factors; (2) the three salient factors identified by previous research are asset specificity, country risk, and firm size; and (3) the degree of integration and new product competitive advantage exert an impact on product market performance.

3. A MODEL OF CHANNEL INTEGRATION IN NEW PRODUCT EXPORT

A model of channel integration in new product export is proposed in Fig. 1. The model links channel integration, antecedents of transaction cost and organizational

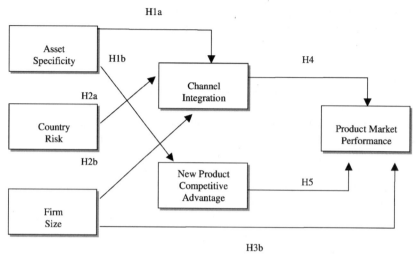

Fig. 1. A Model of Channel Integration in New Product Export: Antecedents and Consequences.

capability, and product market performance. The model includes new product advantage as a contributing factor to product market performance because of its role in enhancing new product performance. The relationships among the constructs in the model are individually developed and hypothesized next.

3.1. Asset Specificity

Asset specificity refers to the extent to which specialized investments and skills are needed to support a transaction (Aulakh & Kotabe, 1997). In new product export, asset specificity pertains to investment in the development of a product, and the skill and proprietary technology required in the development process.

High asset specificity often compels firms to seek options at the upper end of channel integration for several reasons. First, when a firm invests substantially in a new product for export, its stake in the distribution of the product is elevated and extensive efforts are required to achieve product market success. However, foreign distributors may not devote the required efforts because many of them represent several manufacturers and handle multiple lines of competing products. As Bello and Gilliland (1997, p. 26) observe, that "Inattention to a manufacturer's product arises from the goal divergence existing between a distributor carrying many complementary and sometimes competing lines and a manufacturer concerned only with its exported line." This conflict motivates the manufacturer to seek full control of the distribution mechanism which increases chances of product success. Second, products associated with proprietary technology and skills are technically sophisticated and are prone to opportunistic behavior by distributors, which ranges from information leaking to technology piracy. Such behavior creates safeguard problems for firms and causes them to "worry about information leaking via independent channels to actual or potential competitors" (Anderson & Coughlan, 1987, p. 74). Consequently, as proprietary content increases, firms attempt to exert more control to minimize exposure to opportunistic actions by intermediaries.

Third, while several measures are available for curbing middlemen's opportunistic behavior towards products with high asset specificity, these measures generally incur high costs (Lassar & Kerr, 1996). For example, using stringent criteria to screen out unqualified intermediaries increases searching cost prior to contracting. Adding outcome-based incentives to the contract often causes agents to "demand a premium for bearing compensation risk" (Lassar & Kerr, 1996, p. 615). Further, auditing intermediaries for contract implementation raises monitoring cost. As asset specificity increases, the cost associated with these measures will be higher since greater efforts are needed to implement them. The higher cost may be justified when the benefits of these measures are predictable. However, export markets often experience unexpected changes which render the outcomes of these measures unpredictable because "unexpected changes in market demand reduce both partners' ability to predict potential outcomes and render existing contracts incomplete" (Bello & Gilliland, 1997, p. 25). The combination of the high cost and the unpredictability of these measures further reduces the attractiveness of making choices at the lower end of channel integration. Consequently, it is proposed that:

H1a. In new product export, asset specificity increases the level of channel integration.

Asset specificity is also assumed to exert a positive effect on new product competitive advantage. Asset specificity forms an important aspect of the classical theory for product innovation (Kamien & Schwartz, 1982). In the theory, new product advantage is dependent on a firm's specific investment and skills required in developing a new product. Further, the "technology push hypothesis" (Freeman, 1994), a perspective derived from the classical theory, views a firm's specific skills and proprietary technology major determinants of its new product advantage. In export markets, asset specificity is identified as one of the factors that influences product outcomes (Cavusgil & Zou, 1994). Its role stems from the fact that a high level of asset specificity allows a firm to apply advanced features to its products and enhance its distinct capability to meet the requirement of customers in a foreign market. Thus:

H1b. In new product export, asset specificity increases new product competitive advantage.

3.2. Country Risk

Country risk refers to the perceived unpredictability of the political and economic environment in a host country. In export business, country risk is embedded in entry barriers, regulations governing foreign investment, and foreign business tax laws.

High country risk prompts firms to rely less on options at the upper end of channel integration. There are a number of scenarios. In the case of entry barriers, unpredictability of both tariff and non-tariff barriers is adversary to fully owned subsidiaries. A subsidiary's profitability is sensitive to tariffs imposed by governments. An unexpected increase in tariffs poses a threat to a subsidiary because it can turn a subsidiary's profitability into loss. Non-tariff barriers consist of a wide variety, including import quotas, minimum import prices, standard disparities, and proportions restrictions of foreign to domestic goods. Abrupt changes in these barriers can severely disrupt a subsidiary's operations. Because of these potential threats from entry barriers, establishing full control modes in distribution is riskier and less desirable than contracting intermediaries who normally bear the risks associated with tariff and non-tariff barriers.

Government regulations of foreign investment include those guiding foreign ownership, local requirements in ownership, managerial control, prohibition or restrictions of investment in certain sectors. Unpredictability of these regulations poses serious threats to hierarchical distribution channels in foreign markets. For example, a government may allow a fully-owned distribution at the beginning and abruptly change its policy and require local participation in ownership later. A government may also shift its policy from allowing foreign investment in establishing distribution channels to prohibiting investment in certain sections of channel distribution. As a result of these unexpected changes, firms using hierarchical channels for product distribution are either forced to share ownership with local companies or give up their distribution entirely. Therefore, "firms are better off shifting the risk to their independent partners in foreign markets, who are less susceptible to country risk than the foreign export firms (Aulakh & Kotabe, 1997, p. 151)." Based on these arguments, it is proposed that:

H2a. In new product export, country risk reduces the level of channel integration.

Country risk may adversely affect a firm's new product competitive advantage. Uncertainty in tariff and non-tariff barriers can reduce benefits of product advantage. For example, an unexpected increase in tariff will raise the export price of a new product and offset the economic benefits derived from product competitiveness. Moreover, unpredictability in government business regulations can severely erode product advantage. Particularly, when a government is indecisive in enforcing its regulations pertaining technology protection and intellectual property rights, a firm's competitive advantage in technology may be nullified by local competitors' pirated behavior. It is, therefore, proposed that:

H2b. In new product export, country risk reduces new product competitive advantage.

3.3. Firm Size

Firms' capabilities influence their decision of channel modes and ability to implement the decision. While firms with limited capabilities are constrained in making their choices, firms with extended capabilities are endowed with a wide range of selections. According to organizational capability perspective (Aulakh & Kotabe, 1997), firm size is indicative of capabilities since large firms have greater access to resources. In export marketing, firm size is viewed to have a positive relation with the degree of forward integration for several reasons. First, it requires substantial amount of initial capital to establish a subsidiary for product distribution in a foreign market. Large firms have the resources to bear the fixed investment cost required. Second, revenue and profit may not be realized immediately by a newly established subsidiary. Firms with large size have the ability to sustain the cost and the loss associated with the distribution operations. Third, full control modes are preferable for distribution of new products because they are particularly prone to opportunistic behavior by distributors. However, even if companies of lesser sizes prefer full control modes, their decisions are constrained by their limited access to resources. Consequently, they are forced to make choices at the lower end of channel integration. In addition to its effect on channel integration, firm size may also have an impact on new product market performance. A large firm is usually able to commit greater resources to new product marketing activities, such as market research, sales promotion, and product service. Because of the important role of these activities in new product entry success, resource adequacy may offer better opportunities in achieving market results. These discussions lead to the next two hypotheses:

H3a. In new product export, firm size increases the level of channel integration.

H3b. In new product export, firm size enhances new product market performance.

3.4. Channel Integration

According to marketing control perspective (Bello & Gilliland, 1997; Jaworski, 1988), the degree of channel integration exerts an impact on product market performance. In new product export, channel integration plays an important role in performance stimulation. New product performance in a foreign market depends on the control over a series of influencing activities, such as information processing, local selling, retail arrangement, and promoting programs. These activities require focused attention and intensive efforts. In a high vertical integration mode, manufacturers are not only in full control of these activities but also willing to commit the required resources and efforts to these activities. However, in a low control mode, because the key functions are delegated, firms find it hard to coordinate marketing activities for new product introduction and become susceptible to low export performance (Madsen, 1987).

Channel integration also influences product performance through its responsiveness to competition in foreign markets. When a new product is introduced into a foreign market, it is natural for local and foreign competitors to treat it as a threat and adopt strategies to quell its entry. They have a number of options for deterring an entry attempt, including lowering prices of their existing products, introducing imitating substitutes, and rewarding new clients with discounts and better services. Under these competitive pressures, the entrants' speed of response becomes critical for product success. A delayed response to competitors' pricing strategy has negative repercussion on market share. A failure to react to a rival's emulative product may result in losing market leadership. A fully-owned subsidiary can respond to competition more expeditiously than an intermediary for several reasons. First, a subsidiary is better motivated because it has a higher stake in the entry than an intermediary who may carry competing products. Second, a subsidiary is able to devote more efforts in collecting and analyzing competitive information that is essential for swift decision making. Third, an intermediary may lack full autonomy in making key decisions (e.g. product modification), and consequently, consultation with a manufacturing client may further delay market responses.

In addition to competitive response, channel integration affects product performance through a customer information process. New product performance depends on a proper match between new product attributes and target buyers' interest and needs (Griffin & Hauser, 1993). However, a manufacturer cannot achieve such a match without engaging in a process to generate information about customers. This process is particularly relevant in a foreign market where buyer tastes and needs are further complicated by culture and other idiosyncratic factors. A fully-owned subsidiary facilitates the process since it can place marketing personnel in direct contact with markets, intensify interaction with target customers, and speed up integration of local customer information with new product design. This facilitating role is essential in a market where customer tastes and needs shift rapidly. A failure to integrate changes in customer preferences can have detrimental effect on product performance. Hence:

H4. In new product export, the level of channel integration has a positive impact on product market performance.

3.5. New Product Competitive Advantage

Previous research (Calantone & Cooper, 1981; Crawford, 1987; Li & Calantone, 1998; Song & Parry, 1997) in new product development suggests that the presence of product attributes such as newness, reliability, productivity, and uniqueness provides a concrete measure of product competitiveness and differences among products on these attributes offer a direct evidence of advantage.

New product competitive advantage exerts an impact on market performance because of the close relationships between product attributes and buyers' preferences. Traditionally, researchers in marketing assume that customers' preference formation is based on product attributes. When comparing products, buyers generally form favorable perceptions of new products with superior attribute features. They prefer such products both in terms of purchase preferences and actual behavior when the benefits of these features outweigh the costs (Alpert & Kamins, 1995). Empirical studies in new product development provide some evidence that product competitive advantage leads to better market performance. In a study comparing new product performances, Cooper and Kleinschmidt (1987) identify several key product attributes and find that these attributes separate product successes from failures. More recently, Song and Parry (1997, p. 66) review measures of product competitive advantage adopted in previous research and report "a significant positive relationship between the level of new product success and measures of product competitive advantage, such as the presence of unique features, relatively high product quality, and the ability to reduce consumer costs or enable the consumer to perform a unique task." Therefore:

H5. In new product export, new product competitive advantage enhances product market performance.

4. METHOD

4.1. Data Collection

A national database of the U.S. computer software companies was purchased from CorpTech, a commercial data company specializing in high-technology information. The software industry was selected as the research setting for several reasons. First, with a high level of product innovation, the software industry is characterized by frequent new product introductions and various degrees of channel integration in foreign markets. Second, the industry comprises firms serving numerous market segments with highly heterogeneous and non-substitutional software products. As such, each software segment itself meets the criterion of an industry, defined as a group of firms that offers a product or class of products that are close substitutes for each other (Kotler, 1994). Third, the software product allowed us to develop uniform performance measures idiosyncratic to the product and thus simplify the questionnaire form.

From the database, three hundred and seventy-seven companies with export operations were identified. A three-stage procedure was followed to conduct the survey. In the first stage, we sent a personalized letter to presidents/CEOs of the companies in the sampling frame with the research questionnaire and a prepaid envelope. They were requested to identify an executive in the company in charge of new product foreign-market entry and then redirect the research questionnaire to the identified export executive. The second stage consisted of a wave of postcard reminders and a second wave of the survey questionnaires. Finally, a telephone follow-up was conducted among the firms that did not respond. Seven questionnaires were returned undelivered and eleven companies wrote back expressing regret at their inability to participate because of their company policies. From the telephone follow-up, we further learned that thirty-four companies were indirect exporters. Because they exported through domestic export agents (export merchants and export trading companies), they were not qualified to participate. From the remaining pool of three hundred and twenty-eight potential respondents, one hundred and thirty usable responses were received, resulting in a 39.6% response rate.

The informant was asked to concentrate on one foreign country and a software product the company had developed and introduced into that country for a minimum of twelve months and maximum of five years. The informant was requested to answer subsequent questions based on channel decisions and the selected software product. Consistent with Green, Barclay and Ryans (1995), a new product in this study refers to an innovative product in which there is a major functional change to a target market at the time of its entry. A comparison of early and late respondents yielded no significant differences relevant to the study, which suggests that non-response bias is not a problem (Armstrong & Overton, 1977). In regard to sample characteristics, the surveyed soft companies exported to a total of thirty-one different countries and had an average annual sales volume (domestic and foreign) of 75.7 million with an average international sales figures of $26.4 million.

4.2. Measurement

Before testing the hypotheses, we discuss the set of the questionnaire items for each construct in the model. The items were adapted to the setting of new product export from prior research in channel integration, new product development, and export marketing. The complete scales are provided in the Appendix.

Asset Specificity
Asset specificity was measured by three items adapted, in part, from Erramilli and Rao (1993) and Klein, Frazier and Roth (1990). The adaptation was necessary because asset specificity in this study pertains to investment in the development of a new product, and the skill and proprietary technology required in the development process. Following Klein, Frazier and Roth (1990), the items were measured on a seven-point scale ranging from one, "strongly disagree," to seven, "strongly agree" (coefficient alpha = 0.91). For example, the item that "Our investment in developing this software product has been substantial" assessed a firm's investment in the development of a new product. The skill required in the development process was gauged by the item "the skill required to develop this software is highly specialized."

Country Risk
Country risk was measured by three items on a seven-point semantic differential scale (coefficient alpha = 0.84). We adapted these items from previous research (Kim & Hwang, 1992) to assess the respondents' perception of unpredictability of country risk embedded in entry barriers, regulations governing foreign investment, and foreign business tax laws.

Firm size was measured by two indicators, number of employees of the firms and total sales. The two items were converted into a five-point scale for unit uniformity (coefficient alpha = 0.81).

Channel Integration

Respondents were given a description of three major channel options, contractual agreement, joint venture, and wholly-owned subsidiary. These options typify three modes of channel integration: a market mode, an intermediate mode, and a hierarchical mode. In joint venture cases, informants were further offered three types of equity participation: minority ownership, equal ownership, and majority ownership. The further classification of equity participation is necessary since each represents a different level of control (Kim & Hwang, 1992). In contractual agreement cases, respondents were provided with the choices of foreign merchant distributor and commission agent. They were treated as one category because both form their channel relationships with manufacturers through non-equity contractual agreements (Hennart, 1988). Of the one hundred and thirty foreign entry launches used in the analysis, forty-four were wholly-owned-subsidiaries, fifty-five were joint ventures, and thirty-one were contractual agreements. Furthermore, another item that measured level of control was used as a check on channel integration (coefficient alpha = 0.95).

New Product Competitive Advantage

Four product attribute measures (newness, productivity, reliability, uniqueness) were borrowed from Calantone and Cooper (1981), Cooper (1992), and Crawford (1987), who identified these as valid indicators of new product competitiveness. Constructed in a definitional statement (e.g. in terms of newness, i.e. the extent to which a product is new to the market), these items asked respondents to assess their firm's product competitiveness vis-à-vis its largest competitor's with respect to the stated product attributes, using verbal anchors of superiority scale (coefficient alpha = 0.84).

Market Performance

New product market performance was measured by two indicators (coefficient alpha = 0.73). One was a traditional measure of firm's actual product market share in the served market (Buzzell & Gale, 1987). The other was a financial measure of pre-tax profit margin of the new product. The use of these two market performance indicators were justified by the bulk of previous research on new product development (Griffin & Page, 1993).

As a test of discriminant validity of these measures, we used a procedure recommended by Bagozzi, Yi and Phillips (1991). Within each subset of measures, pairs

Table 1. Discriminant Analysis.

Constructs	χ^2	df	$\Delta\chi^{2a}$
Antecedents			
Asset Specificity (F1) vs. Country Risk (F2)			
Unconstrained	16.26	10	256.50
Constrained	272.75	11	
Asset Specificity (F1) vs. Firm Size (F3)			
Unconstrained	10.79	6	148.96
Constrained	159.75	7	
Country Risk (F2) vs. Firm Size (F3)			
Unconstrained	12.91	6	168.10
Constrained	181.01	7	
Contributory Factors			
Channel Integration (F4) vs. Competitive Advantage (F5)			
Unconstrained	27.46	10	251.34
Constrained	278.80	11	

[a] The $\Delta\chi^2$ were all significant ($p < 0.01$).

of constructs were assessed in a series of two-factor confirmatory models using EQS. For example, the set of measures of asset specificity was paired with the set of country risk. We ran each model twice – once constraining the correlation between the two constructs to unity and once freeing the parameter. Then a chi-square difference test was conducted. As shown in Table 1, the chi-square value for the unconstrained model was 16.26 (df = 10), significant lower than the constrained model's 272.75 (df = 11), suggesting discriminant validity of the two constructs. Further, as shown in the test between country risk and firm size, the unconstrained model yields a chi-square value of 12.91 (df = 6), significantly lower than the constrained model's 181.01. The chi-square differences for all other pairs of constructs were also significant, providing evidence supporting construct differentiation.

4.3. Measurement Model

We conducted a confirmatory factor analysis (CFA) through EQS (Bentler, 1989) to assess the measurement model using the covariance matrix in Table 2 as input. In Table 3, we show the results of the measurement model that employs sixteen indicators for the six constructs. The fit of the CFA model is acceptable. The chi-square for the CFA is 122.08 (df 91, $p < 0.017$), indicating small ratio between the chi-square and the degrees of freedom. The Normed Fit Index (NFI),

Table 2. Variance-Covariance Matrix.

	$Spec_1$	$Spec_2$	$Spec_3$	$Risk_1$	$Risk_2$	$Risk_3$	$Size_1$	$Size_2$	$Chan_1$	$Chan_2$	$Advn_1$	$Advn_2$	$Advn_3$	$Advn_4$	$Perf_1$	$Perf_2$
$Spec_1$	1.87															
$Spec_2$	1.55	2.17														
$Spec_3$	1.67	1.66	2.17													
$Risk_1$	−0.55	−0.48	−0.51	1.55												
$Risk_2$	−0.45	−0.56	−0.45	0.91	1.69											
$Risk_3$	−0.62	−0.66	−0.64	0.95	1.09	1.38										
$Size_1$	0.18	−0.07	0.22	−0.23	−0.26	−0.25	1.81									
$Size_2$	0.31	0.04	0.24	−0.43	−0.37	−0.37	1.57	2.77								
$Chan_1$	0.87	0.70	0.75	−0.52	−0.66	−0.62	0.46	0.84	2.60							
$Chan_2$	0.77	0.62	0.67	−0.36	−0.49	−0.48	0.32	0.66	2.15	2.11						
$Advn_1$	0.41	0.43	0.58	−0.42	−0.56	−0.41	0.26	0.28	0.42	0.24	1.49					
$Advn_2$	0.30	0.34	0.42	−0.41	−0.46	−0.46	0.27	0.31	0.57	0.50	0.82	1.44				
$Advn_3$	0.42	0.33	0.40	−0.47	−0.49	−0.26	0.09	0.30	0.51	0.35	0.89	0.80	1.58			
$Advn_4$	0.42	0.40	0.50	−0.45	−0.46	−0.36	0.08	0.25	0.46	0.38	0.71	0.89	0.89	1.25		
$Perf_1$	0.73	0.57	0.78	−0.55	−0.51	−0.45	0.22	0.91	1.06	0.80	0.39	0.32	0.51	0.44	2.32	
$Perf_2$	0.56	0.49	0.55	−0.48	−0.58	−0.52	0.38	0.63	0.73	0.51	0.73	0.62	0.81	0.65	1.16	1.68
μ	4.19	4.20	4.40	2.77	2.61	2.39	2.32	2.50	3.10	3.04	4.89	5.00	4.71	5.17	3.32	3.59
s	1.47	1.48	1.37	1.25	1.30	1.18	1.35	1.67	1.61	1.45	1.22	1.20	1.26	1.12	1.53	1.30

Table 3.   Construct Measurement Summary: Confirmatory Factor Analysis and Scale Reliability.

Constructs	Indicators	Standardized Item-construct Loading	t-Value
Asset Specificity F1 ($\alpha = 0.91$)	$Spec_1$	0.92	13.54
	$Spec_2$	0.84	15.39
	$Spec_3$	0.90	
Country Risk F2 ($\alpha = 0.84$)	$Risk_1$	0.73	8.41
	$Risk_2$	0.79	8.84
	$Risk_3$	0.89	
Firm Size F3 ($\alpha = 0.81$)	$Size_1$	0.72	11.04
	$Size_2$	0.97	
Channel Integration F4 ($\alpha = 0.95$)	$Chan_1$	0.98	26.27
	$Chan_2$	0.94	
New Product Competitive Advantage F5 ($\alpha = 0.84$)	$Advn_1$	0.71	7.85
	$Advn_2$	0.77	7.82
	$Advn_3$	0.76	8.26
	$Advn_4$	0.82	
Product Market Performance F6 ($\alpha = 0.73$)	$Perf_1$	0.69	6.60
	$Perf_2$	0.85	

Note: $\chi^2_{(91)} = 122.08, p = 0.02$; NFI $= 0.91$; NNFI $= 0.96$; CFI $= 0.97$; AOSR $= 0.03$; LSR $= 0.13$ (96% between $- 0.1$ and 0.1).

the Non-normed Fit Index (NNFI), and the Comparative Fit Index (CFI) are 0.91, 0.96, and 0.97 respectively. The average off-diagonal standardized residual (AOSR) is 0.04. CFI is used as the primary index to evaluate the model since "the mean of the sampling distribution of NFI is positively associated with sample size and the NFI substantially underestimates its asymptotic value at small sample sizes" (Hu & Bentler, 1995, p. 89). Furthermore, the indicators have large and significant loadings on their posited construct showing convergent validity. Overall, the results suggest that the model represents an adequate fit to the data.

4.4. Structural Model

The proposed structural model was specified from the hypothesized relationships shown in Fig. 1. The hypotheses were tested by using maximum likelihood estimation in EQS. As shown in Fig. 2, the chi-square statistic for the model

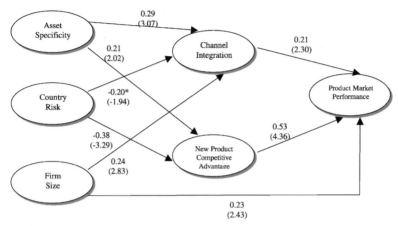

Fig. 2. Structural Model Estimates. *Note:* $\chi^2_{(95)} = 128.62$, $p = 0.01$; NFI = 0.90; NNFI = 0.96; CFI = 0.97; AOSR = 0.04; LSR = 0.16 (93% between $\chi - 0.1$ and 0.1). * Not significant.

is 128.62 (df = 95, $p = 0.012$) showing small ratio between the chi-square and degrees of freedom. CFI is 0.97 and AOSR is small with a value of 0.04. NFI and NNFI are 0.90 and 0.96 indicating acceptability. Based on these results, we feel that the model represents an adequate fit to the data.

Next, we evaluated our structural model using the procedure recommended by Anderson and Gerbing (1988). We compared our focal hypothesized model (a restricted theoretical model, M_t) with a less constrained alternative model (M_u). Two tests were conducted. In the first test, we relaxed M_u by freeing the path from asset specificity to product market performance. A chi-square difference test (CDT) was used to test the null hypothesis: $M_t - M_u = 0$. The chi-square difference (M_t has a χ^2 of 128.62 and 95 df and M_u has a χ^2 of 125.82 and 94 df) is 2.80 at $p = 0.10$. The non-significant CDT suggests an acceptance of M_t. In the second test, we relaxed the path from country risk to product market performance from zero and freed it to be estimated. This time, M_u resulted in a χ^2 of 126.51 with 95 df. The chi-square difference between M_t and M_u is 2.11 at $p = 0.15$, again indicating an acceptance of M_t. Thus, our restricted theoretical model is preferred to the less restricted competing model.

The standardized parameter estimates and corresponding t-values are shown in Fig. 2. The results are as follows.

- **For H1,** as hypothesized: (a) asset specificity increases the level of channel integration ($b = 0.29$, $t = 3.07$, $p < 0.01$); and (b) asset specificity increases new product competitive advantage ($b = 0.21$, $t = 2.02$, $p < 0.05$).

- **For H2a**, although there appears to be a negative relationship between country risk and the level of channel integration ($b = -0.20$, $t = -1.94$, $p < 0.05$), the results are not statistically significant.
- **For H2b**, as proposed, country risk has a negative impact on new product competitive advantage ($b = -0.38$, $t = -3.29$, $p < 0.01$).
- **For H3**, as hypothesized, (a) firm size increases the level of channel integration ($b = 0.24$, $t = 2.83$, $p < 0.01$), and (b) firm size enhances new product market performance ($b = 0.23$, $t = 2.43$, $p < 0.01$).
- **H4** is supported. The level of channel integration enhances new product market performance ($b = 0.21$, $t = 2.30$, $p < 0.05$).
- **For H5**, as proposed, new product competitive advantage enhances new product market performance ($b = 0.53$, $t = 4.36$, $p < 0.01$).

5. DISCUSSION AND IMPLICATIONS

5.1. Findings

In this study, we develop a conceptual model of channel integration in new product export. We propose that both the degree of channel integration and new product competitive advantage exert a positive impact on product market performance. We further conduct a test using data collected from the software industry. The results provide evidence supporting our central propositions. Specifically, product market performance is found to be determined in part by the degree of channel integration and in part by the level of new product competitive advantage. Of the two contributing factors, new product competitive advantage appears to exert a stronger impact on product performance since it has a larger standardized coefficient ($b = 0.53$, $t = 4.36$). This finding suggests that product competitive advantage plays an essential role in enhancing product performance in export markets. Although channel integration displays a somewhat lesser role, its effect on product performance is substantial ($b = 0.21$, $t = 2.30$). This finding is significant because it provides evidence linking, directly, the degree of channel integration with product performance. This linkage was not documented previously.

Our research also investigates the relationships between the antecedents of transaction cost and channel integration. The results show that asset specificity influences the degree of channel integration. Specifically, we find that asset specificity is positively correlated with the degree of channel integration ($b = 0.29$, $t = 3.07$). Apparently, as firms invest heavily in new product development for export, they intend to make choices at the upper end of channel integration that provides better control of distribution mechanism. This finding may also suggest that when firms develop products with special skills and high proprietary technology, they want to exert more control to minimize exposures to opportunistic actions by intermediaries. This is consistent with Anderson and Coughlan (1987) who observe that firms with special investment in asset worry about information leaking via independent channels to actual or potential competitors. The results show the negative impact of country risk on the degree of channel integration is not significant statistically ($b = -20, t = -1.94$). The literature assumes that as entry barriers and foreign investment regulations become unpredictable, firms prefer options as the lower end of channel integration. However, the finding does not confirm the view in the literature and it is unclear whether it is a dominant practice for firms to shift the risk to independent partners under uncertain conditions.

The findings about the effect of asset specificity and country risk on new product competitive advantage are noteworthy. Asset specificity is found to exert a positive impact on new product competitive advantage ($b = 0.21, t = 2.02$). This finding suggests that a firm needs to develop special skills and proprietary technology to enhance its product competitiveness in the market place. This finding is significant because it expands the role of asset specificity in channel research. The results also show that country risk has a significant negative influence on new product competitive advantage ($b = -0.38, t = -3.29$). This finding highlights the importance of identifying a country with a stable business environment for foreign investment. A firm's competitive advantage can be nullified in a country with unpredictable government regulations.

The results also show that firm size is positively correlated with the level of channel integration ($b = 0.24, t = 2.83$). This finding suggests an inclination of large firms in making selections at the upper end of channel integration in new product export. It may also indicate that large firms have better access to resources that are needed in establishing their own distribution networks. Additionally, the results provide evidence supporting the relationship between firm size and product market performance ($b = 0.23, t = 2.43$). This finding seems to demonstrate the positive role of firm size in new product entry into foreign markets. Because extensive marketing efforts are required for new product success, firms that are able to commit resources in carrying out these efforts have better chances in achieving goals.

5.2. Managerial Implications

This research provides management responsible for new product export with a better understanding of the effectiveness of channel integration. The results show that in new product entry, high control modes have a positive impact on market performance. This is a significant finding since previous research (Aulakh & Kotabe, 1997) suggests that degree of channel integration is not related to performance. In light of this finding, firms need to seriously consider using a fully-owned subsidiary or a joint venture for new product introduction in foreign markets. The high control modes are effective because they allow firms to fully conduct marketing activities, such as information processing, retail arrangement, and promotion programs. Furthermore, these control modes directly connect firms with the market and permit them to respond to their customers and competitors more swiftly than low control modes. It should also be noted that some firms are prohibited from establishing high control modes in their initial foreign market entry because of limited resources. However, they should consider switching modes when their resource capability strengthens. Our managerial implication is consistent with the theory of export involvement (Douglas & Craig, 1989). The theory views export commitment as an evolutionary process consisting of three stages: the pre-involvement stage, the reactive involvement stage, and the active involvement stage. In the third stage, high control modes in distribution become necessary because the firm commits itself to foreign markets and invests heavily in developing new products for customers in foreign markets.

The observed negative effect of country risk on new product competitive advantage has implications for country risk management. Although country risk analysis is an important aspect of foreign market assessment in international business management, its specific impact on new product entry into foreign markets was not well understood previously. The results of this study show country risk adversely affects new product entry through reducing the level of new product competitive advantage. Hence, a thorough analysis of country risk needs to be conducted by firms that contemplate introducing new products into foreign markets. Because country risk may erode the inherent competitiveness in new products, firms should avoid entering markets with potentially high risk. Choosing a country with high risk is not only detrimental to the firm in regard to its product competitive advantage, but also pernicious to its product market performance.

The observed positive correlation between asset specificity and the level of channel integration should be assessed jointly with the impact of channel integration on performance. The results show that firms with heavy investment in new product development generally adopt high control modes as a strategy to protect their investment. This approach proves to be effective since high control modes are found to enhance new product performance in the market. Consequently, when firms develop export products with special skills and proprietary technology, they should use high control modes in their attempt to fully realize the potential of their investment. In addition to its influence on channel integration, asset specificity is also found to exert a positive impact on product competitive advantage. This finding highlights the importance of developing skills and technology specific to the needs of foreign markets. This is in contrast with the standardization approach that views developing standardized products for multiple country markets as an effective way to increase the economies of scale in global market. While standardization stresses benefits from cost savings, firms that intend to build product competitiveness should center on honing technical skills specific to a market.

5.3. Future Research

Certain limitations in this study provide opportunities for future research. First, the research setting in this study is necessarily restricted to the computer software industry. While the multi-industry characteristic of our research setting increases the generalizability of the findings, this cannot be exaggerated since the findings may be skewed to the channel distribution of high-tech and information intensive products. This limitation may be overcome in the future through a comparative study involving different industries. Additionally, comparative studies may lead to new research topics. For example, what is the impact of industry characteristics on channel integration? Samiee and Roth (1992) classify global industries into two groups, one marked by rapid technological change and the other by technological stability. Do firms operating in the two groups require different levels of channel integration? Additionally, our sample consists only of U.S. firms having foreign distribution channels. Therefore, the external validity of our findings is not readily applicable to firms based in other countries. A future investigation using surveys of high-tech export firms in other countries will address this limitation and test the empirical generalizability of the findings from this research.

Second, this research does not investigate the relationships between channel integration and speed in product introduction. In recent years, speed in new product introduction to foreign markets has become a critical dimension of competition among firms in high-technology industries (Craig & Hart, 1992; Yeoh, 1994). Companies are particularly interested in two issues: (1) how to enter a market ahead of competitors; and (2) how to maintain market position after the entry. While the first relates to the topic of being the first mover in a new product market, the second involves preserving the first mover advantage. We believe that an integration of channel studies with research on entry speed will provide insight to theses issues. For example, a high control mode may help a firm execute its first mover strategy by providing swift intelligence on competitors' development speed and intentions. On the other hand, a low control mode may delay the delivery of customer information and thus hinder a timely entry to foreign markets.

Third, this study does not examine global standardization strategy. This leaves an intriguing topic for future research: the role of channel integration in implementation of global standardization strategy. Global product standardization represents an important research stream in international management (Jain, 1989; Levitt, 1983; Yip, 1989). However, the findings from empirical studies (Boddewyn, Soehl & Picard, 1986; Samiee & Roth, 1992) show standardization results were heterogeneous with standardization exerting both positive and negative impact on market performance. Channel integration studies may contribute to research on global standardization strategy by offering explanation for its heterogeneous performance. Theoretically, channel control may play a role in moderating the relationships between standardization strategy and performance. Because standardization success depends on coordinated efforts across markets in multiple countries, effective control of distribution channels in different countries is essential in coordinating those efforts. As a result, firms that are in better control of distribution channel are more likely to reach performance goals with standardization strategy than those in less control. In sum, integration of research on channel integration with studies of global strategy may advance research in both areas.

REFERENCES

Agarwal, S., & Ramaswami, S. N. (1992). Choice of foreign market entry mode: Impact of ownership, location, and internalization factors. *Journal of International Business Studies, 23*(1), 1–27.

Alpert, F. H., & Kamins, M. A. (1995). An empirical investigation of consumer memory, attitude, and perceptions toward pioneer and follower brands. *Journal of Marketing, 59*(4), 34–45.

Anderson, E., & Coughlan, A. T. (1987). International market entry and expansion via independent or integrated channels of distribution. *Journal of Marketing, 51*(1), 71–82.

Anderson, E., & Gatignon, H. (1986). Modes of foreign entry: A transaction cost analysis and propositions. *Journal of International Business Studies, 17*(4), 1–26.

Anderson, J. C., & Gerbing, D. W. (1988). Structural equation modeling in practice: A review and recommended two-step approach. *Psychological Bulletin, 103*(4), 411–423.

Armstrong, J. S., & Overton, T. S. (1977). Estimating nonresponse bias in mail surveys. *Journal of Marketing Research, 16*(3), 396–400.

Atuahene-Gima, K. (1995). The influence of new product factors on export propensity and performance: An empirical analysis. *Journal of International Marketing, 3*(2), 11–28.

Aulakh, P. S., & Kotabe, M. (1997). Antecedents and performance implications of channel integration in foreign markets. *Journal of International Business Studies, 28*(1), 145–175.

Bagozzi, R., Yi, Y., & Phillips, L. W. (1991). Assessing construct validity in organizational research. *Administrative Science Quarterly, 36*, 421–458.

Bello, D. C., & Gilliland, D. I. (1997). The effect of output controls, process controls, and flexibility on export channel performance. *Journal of Marketing, 61*(1), 22–38.

Bentler, P. M. (1989). *EQS structural equations program manual*. Los Angeles: BMDP Statistical Software.

Boddewyn, J. J., Soehl, R., & Picard, J. (1986). Standardization in international marketing: Is Ted Levitt in fact right? *Business Horizons, 29*(6), 69–75.

Buzzell, R., & Gale, B. T. (1987). *The PIMS principles: Linking strategy to performance*. New York: Free Press.

Calantone, R. J., & Cooper, R. G. (1981). New product scenarios: Prospects for success. *Journal of Marketing, 45*(1), 48–60.

Cavusgil, S. T. (1988). Unraveling the mystique of export pricing. *Business Horizons, 31*(May–June), 54–63.

Cavusgil, S. T., & Kirpalani, V. H. (1993). Introducing products into export markets: Success factors. *Journal of Business Research, 27*(1), 1–15.

Cavusgil, S. T., & Zou, S. (1994). Marketing strategy-performance relationship: An investigation of the empirical link in export market ventures. *Journal of Marketing, 58*(1), 1–21.

Cooper, R. G. (1992). The newprod system: The industry experience. *Journal of Product Innovation Management, 9*(2), 113–127.

Cooper, R. G., & Kleinschmidt, E. J. (1987). New products: What separates winners and losers? *Journal of Product Innovation Management, 4*(3), 169–184.

Craig, A., & Hart, S. (1992). Where to now in new product development research? *European Journal of Marketing, 26*(11), 1–49.

Crawford, C. M. (1987). *New products management*. Homewood, IL: Irwin.

Day, G. S. (1994). The capabilities of market-driven organizations. *Journal of Marketing, 58*(4), 37–52.

Douglas, S. P., & Craig, C. S. (1989). Evolution of global marketing strategy: Scale, scope, and synergy. *Columbia Journal of World Business, 24*(Fall), 47–59.

Erramilli, M. K., & Rao, C. P. (1993). Service firms' international entry mode choice: A modified transaction-cost analysis approach. *Journal of Marketing, 57*(3), 9–38.

Freeman, C. (1994). The economics of technical change. *Cambridge Journal of Economics, 18,* 463–514.

Green, D. H., Barclay, D. W., & Ryans, A. B. (1995). Entry strategy and long-term performance: Conceptualization and empirical examination. *Journal of Marketing, 59*(4), 1–16.

Griffin, A., & Hauser, J. R. (1993). The voice of the customer. *Marketing Science, 12*(1), 1–27.

Griffin, A., & Page, A. L. (1993). An interim report on measuring product development success and failure. *Journal of Product Innovation Management, 10*(4), 291–308.

Hennart, J. F. (1988). A transaction costs theory of equity joint ventures. *Strategic Management Journal, 9*(3), 361–374.

Hu, L., & Bentler, P. M. (1995). Evaluating model fit. In: R. H. Hoyle (Ed.), *Structural Equation Modeling* (pp. 76–99). Thousand Oaks, CA: Sage Publications.

Jain, S. (1989). Standardization of international marketing strategy: Some research hypotheses. *Journal of Marketing, 53*(1), 70–79.

Jaworski, B. J. (1988). Toward a theory of marketing control: Environmental context, control types, and consequences. *Journal of Marketing, 52*(3), 23–39.

Kamien, M. I., & Schwartz, N. L. (1982). *Market structure and innovation*. Cambridge: Cambridge University Press.

Kim, W. C., & Hwang, P. (1992). Global strategy and multinationals' entry mode choice. *Journal of International Business Studies, 23*(1), 29–53.

Klein, S., Frazier, G. L., & Roth, V. J. (1990). A transaction cost analysis model of channel integration in international markets. *Journal of Marketing Research, 27*(2), 196–208.

Kotler, P. (1994). *Marketing management*. Englewood Cliffs, NJ: Prentice-Hall.

Lassar, W. M., & Kerr, J. (1996). Strategy and control in supplier distributor relationships: An agency perspective. *Strategic Management Journal, 17*, 613–632.

Lawrence, P. R., & Lorsch, J. W. (1967). *Organization and environment: Managing differentiation and integration*. Homewood, IL: Irwin.

Levitt, T. (1983). The globalization of markets. *Harvard Business Review, 61*(3), 92–102.

Li, T., & Calantone, R. J. (1998). The impact of market knowledge competence on new product advantage: Conceptualization and empirical examination. *Journal of Marketing, 62*(4), 13–29.

Madhok, A. (1997). Cost, value and foreign market entry mode. *Strategic Management Journal, 18*(1), 39–61.

Madsen, T. K. (1987). Empirical export performance studies: A review of conceptualization and findings. *Advances in International Marketing, 2*, 177–198.

Samiee, S., & Roth, K. (1992). The influence of global marketing standardization on performance. *Journal of Marketing, 56*(2), 1–17.

Song, X. M., & Parry, M. E. (1997). The determinants of Japanese new product successes. *Journal of Marketing Research, 34*(1), 64–76.

Williamson, O. E. (1975). *Markets and hierarchies: Analysis and antitrust implications*. New York: Free Press.

Williamson, O. E. (1985). *The economic institutions of capitalism*. New York: Free Press.

Yeoh, P. L. (1994). Speed to global markets: An empirical prediction of new product success in the ethical pharmaceutical industry. *European Journal of Marketing, 28*(11), 29–49.

Yip, G. S. (1989). Global strategy. In a world of nations? *Sloan Management Review, 31*(4), 29–41.

APPENDIX

Construct Measures

Asset Specificity (F1)

$Spec_1$ Our investment in developing this software product has been substantial.

$Spec_2$ The skill required to develop this software is highly specialized.

$Spec_3$ The technology required to develop this software is proprietary.
            (scale: 1 = strongly disagree to 7 = strongly agree)

Country Risk (F2)

$Risk_1$ Tariff/Non-tariff barriers in this foreign country are highly predictable/highly unpredictable.

$Risk_2$ Government regulations regarding foreign investment in this foreign country are highly predictable/highly unpredictable.

$Risk_3$ Foreign business tax laws in this foreign country are highly predictable/highly unpredictable.
            (scale: 1 = highly predictable to 7 = highly unpredictable)

APPENDIX *(Continued)*

Firm Size (F3)

Size₁ Number of employees of the firm (converted into 5-point scale: <100, 100–200, 201–300, 301–400, >400).

Size₂ Total sales of the firm (converted into 5-point scale: <$25 million, $25–50 million, $50–75 million, $75–100 million, >$100 million).

Channel Integration (F4)

Chan₁ Which of the following best describes the distribution channel of your new software product in the foreign market you have entered?
  1. Contractual agreement
     a. Foreign merchant distributor
     b. Commission agent
  2. Joint venture with local partner (minority ownership)
  3. Joint venture with local partner (equal ownership)
  4. Joint venture with local partner (majority ownership)
  5. Wholly owned subsidiary
  Other (specify)

Chan₂ Our control over the distribution of this software product in this country is low/high.
  (scale: 1 = low to 5 = high).

New Product Competitive Advantage (F5)

How would you compare your software product with your competitors products in this foreign market? Our software is not superior at all/extremely superior:

Advn₁ in terms of newness, i.e. the extent to which a product is new to the market.

Advn₂ in terms of productivity, i.e. the extent to which a software increases a customer's work efficiency.

Advn₃ in terms of reliability, i.e. the extent to which a software is free of error.

Advn₄ in terms of uniqueness, i.e. the extent to which a software has unique functions.
  (scale: 1 = not superior at all to 7 = extremely superior).

Product Market Performance (F6)

Perf₁ Product market share (percentage converted into 5-point scale: 1–5%, 6–10%; 11–15%, 16–20%, >21%).

Perf₂ Pre-tax profit margin on this product (percentage converted into 5-point scale: 1–5%, 6–10%; 11–15%, 16–20%, >21%).

GRAY MARKETS: THREAT OR OPPORTUNITY? THE CASE OF HERMAN MILLER v. ASAL GmbH

Michael R. Mullen, C. M. Sashi and Patricia M. Doney

ABSTRACT

Market entry strategies range from foreign direct investment to licensing with varying levels of commitment, risk and opportunity. Exporting products or services is one of the most common of the intermediate market entry strategies. It is typically accomplished through authorized international channels of distribution. However, when significant price differences exist between markets, alternative, parallel channels of distribution are almost certain to arise. These parallel channels, often referred to as gray marketing, are generally legal but unauthorized distribution channels that create an alternative export market entry. After a review of the literature, a case study highlights these complex issues from the perspective of both manufacturer and parallel marketer. The case study provides a tool for evaluating theory and a basis for discussing this important alternative mode of market entry. The case and the discussion which follows also highlight the role of international trade shows as an important element of the marketing mix for entering many foreign markets.

Reviving Traditions in Research on International Market Entry
Advances in International Marketing, Volume 14, 77–105
© 2003 Published by Elsevier Science Ltd.
ISSN: 1474-7979/doi:10.1016/S1474-7979(03)14005-7

INTRODUCTION

The globalization of markets is not a new phenomenon but one that has accelerated in recent years. Firms must decide where, when and how to enter foreign markets if they are to remain competitive. The issue of how to enter foreign markets is often referred to as the mode of entry. Market entry strategies range from foreign direct investment to licensing with varying levels of commitment, risk and opportunity. Exporting products or services is one of the most common of the intermediate market entry strategies (Root, 1994). It is typically accomplished through authorized international channels of distribution (for recent reviews, see Mullen, 1990, Mullen et al., 1999). These international channels of distribution may include contractual, administrative, corporate or collaborative relationships with foreign sales reps, distributors, retail outlets, Internet Service Providers and/or other intermediaries.

Along with the globalization of markets, the convergence or homogenization of consumer demand has led many firms to follow Levitt's (1983) advice to produce and market the same products the same way everywhere. Examples of such products include Coke and Pepsi-Cola, Levi's jeans, Parker pens, Seiko and Swatch watches, Duracell batteries, Opium perfume, Olympus, Nikon and Minolta cameras, Sony car stereos, BMW, VW and Mercedes-Benz cars, and Caterpillar tractors. However, these "global products" are often sold at very different prices in different markets. In a recent study, KPMG Consulting surveyed retail prices for thirty-three directly comparable products in twelve EU countries. They found that twenty-nine of the thirty-three products showed price differentials of more than 50% between the highest and lowest-priced countries. Fifteen of thirty-three had price gaps of 100% or more (Kotabe & Helsen, 2001).

When significant price differences exist between markets for nearly identical products, alternative, parallel channels of distribution are almost certain to appear. These parallel channels are often referred to as gray marketing. According to Duhan and Sheffet (1988), gray marketing "involves the selling of trademarked goods through channels of distribution that are not authorized by the trademark holder." Gray markets arise when genuine products are sold by intermediaries other than the distribution channel authorized by the trademark owner in a market. "Gray marketers are typically brokers who buy goods overseas, either from manufacturers or authorized dealers, at relatively low prices and import them into a country where prevailing prices are higher" (Cavusgil & Sikora, 1988, p. 75).

Gray markets are a worldwide phenomenon with multinational companies that market products globally in different countries increasingly susceptible to diversion of merchandise into parallel channels of distribution. The emergence of global products that are almost identical everywhere and backed by global advertising strategies has exacerbated the problem for multinational companies (Assmus & Wiese, 1995). International gray marketers play a significant role in bringing products to discount stores and ultimately to consumers at low prices (Chen, 2002). Kiyak (1997) estimated the total gray market at $15 billion in 1994, with market shares of 25–30% in some industries. However, the size of the gray market varies by industry and country. Estimates of products sold by parallel channels in the United States alone range between $7 billion and $10 billion (Ball et al., 2002; Cespedes, Corey & Rangan, 1988). For instance, Canadian auto dealers take advantage of lower invoice prices and fluctuating exchange rates to send an estimated 200,000 vehicles South of the border annually (*Automotive News*, 2002). In the EU, the gray market ranges from 2 to 10% of the total market for prescription medicine (Chaudhry & Walsh, 1995) while 80% of U.K. high tech distributors are believed to be selling gray market computer drives (Kunert, 2002). While data on gray markets are hard to find for emerging markets, one article notes price differentials of at least 20% in India for telecom handsets and the existence of huge gray markets in emerging markets (Sharma, 2002). Manufacturers and their authorized channel members in the United States have sought judicial and regulatory assistance to eliminate parallel channels of distribution, viewing parallel channels as a threat and using the pejorative label "gray marketing."

The complex nature and magnitude of the problem have made parallel channels of distribution and gray marketing the subject of many academic articles (see following review), international business textbooks (Ball et al., 2002; Czinkota, Rivoli & Ronkainen, 1992; Daniels & Radebaugh, 2001; Hill, 2001; Punnett & Ricks, 1992), and international marketing textbooks (Cateora & Graham, 2002; Czinkota & Ronkainen, 1990; Johansson, 2003; Keegan, 2002; Keegan & Green, 2003; Kotabe & Helsen, 2001; Onkvisit & Shaw, 1997). These articles and texts contain many examples and vignettes, but no case studies appropriate for explicating these complex issues.

Purpose

The main purposes of this manuscript are to highlight issues concerning parallel channels of distribution as an alternative mode of entry and present a case study that helps us evaluate theory using field observation. Case studies of parallel channels and gray marketing are rare.[1] Multinational firms are reluctant to openly discuss the specifics from their firm's perspective because of the strategic and legal issues involved. To address this void, we gathered data from public records to develop a topical case study that gives students of international business and marketing a chance to analyze the creation of an international parallel channel of distribution from several perspectives: that of the manufacturer, authorized distributors in different territories, and the gray market entrepreneurs that attempt to arbitrage price differentials between the U.S. and European markets. Thus, students can consider a "gray market" situation as a threat or opportunity and compare theory and practice.[2] The case also addresses the role of international trade shows as an important promotional aspect of international market entry. Finally, the discussion and appendix are intended to provide information that might be helpful to managers and students of international marketing.

Organization

In the two-part literature review which follows, we first discuss legal issues, i.e. efforts of trademark owners seeking to protect their authorized channel members. Then, following the case study methodology proposed by Perry (1998), we review the relevant literature on parallel channels of distribution and gray marketing to identify research issues and present a theoretical framework developed from the literature review. Next the case of Herman Miller v. ASAL GmbH is presented, followed by a discussion that addresses theoretical and managerial issues and implications. Based on facts of the case, the expanded role of international trade shows is also discussed in some detail. The short conclusion is followed by an appendix providing an update on the Herman Miller v. ASAL GmbH case.

LEGAL ISSUES CONCERNING
PARALLEL CHANNELS

Parallel channels of distribution have had a long and controversial legal history. The legality of the product itself is not in question and it is neither counterfeit nor fake. However, the legality of the means by which the product is distributed falls in a gray area between legal and illegal marketing activities that vary across time and jurisdictions (Duhan & Sheffet, 1988).

The legal status of parallel channels has largely been determined by case law in the United States. An early decision that set a precedent followed for almost four decades was *Appolinaris Co., Ltd. v. Scherer* (1886). The plaintiff had an exclusive agreement with a Hungarian producer to distribute Hunyadi Janos mineral water in the U.S., but the defendant imported the water from an authorized German distributor and sold it in the U.S. The court ruled that the product was genuine and hence no infringement of the trademark had occurred, establishing the principle of universality, which treats the trademark only as indication of the source or origin of the product. It was not until *A. Bourjois & Co. v. Katzel* (1923) that the principle of territoriality emerged by which a U.S. trademark owner can stop gray marketing because products bearing that trademark are under the U.S. trademark owner's control within the U.S. The plaintiff in the case had purchased the exclusive right to sell a French face powder named Java in the U.S. but the defendant bought the product in France and began importing and selling it in the U.S. The lower court ruled that the plaintiff had the exclusive right to use the trademark Java in the U.S., but the Second Court of Appeals reversed the decision on the grounds that the product was genuine. This decision was in turn reversed by the Supreme Court which held that the plaintiff had advertised and established in the eyes of the public that it was the source of Java in the United States even though it did not manufacture the product but only distributed it.

Subsequent interpretations by the Customs Service charged with enforcing these laws culminated in two cases heard by two different U.S. appeals courts that came to opposite conclusions, prompting the Supreme Court to hear the cases on appeal (Cross, Stephens & Benjamin, 1990). In *Coalition to Preserve the Integrity of American Trademarks (COPIAT) v. U.S.* (1986), a trade association of U.S. trademark owners with foreign licensees allowed to manufacture and distribute the products only in foreign countries sought to bar the importation of these products by K-Mart, which purchased them abroad from one of the licensee's distributors. The court ruled that Customs Service regulations that deny protection when there is a connection between the manufacturer and distributor were invalid and the goods should be barred. But in *Olympus Corp. v. U.S.* (1986), an action brought by the U.S. subsidiary of a Japanese camera manufacturer to bar K-Mart from importing and selling Olympus products bought from a distributor in a foreign market, another appeals court upheld the lower court's opinion that the Customs Service interpretation allowing entry was valid. The Supreme Court's decision divided the gray market issue into three cases: (1) Unrelated purchase where a U.S. firm purchases from a foreign manufacturer the right to distribute trademarked goods in the United States when unauthorized importation of the trademarked good is barred; (2) Affiliated firms in which the foreign manufacturer and domestic firm that owns the trademark are under common control when unauthorized importation of the trademarked good is permitted; and (3) Authorized use where a foreign manufacturer is authorized by a U.S. manufacturer to produce a trademarked good when unauthorized importation of the trademarked good is barred (Cross, Stephens & Benjamin, 1990). Thus, gray market activity is curtailed in the case of unrelated purchase and authorized use, but permitted in the case of affiliated firms. The latter decision affirms the appeals court decision in the Olympus case and reverses the appeals court decision in the COPIAT case.

Recent rulings by the European Court of Justice (ECJ) in two landmark decisions are expected to significantly influence the appearance of parallel channels and gray market activity in the expanding European Union and the European Economic Area (the EU members plus Iceland, Norway, and Lichtenstein). In the very near future, ten to thirteen additional nations are expected join the EU, enlarging the membership to at least twenty-five and possibly twenty-eight total nations with as many as five hundred and forty-five million people (European Commission, 2002).

In *Silhouette International Schmied GmbH & Co. KG v. Hartlauer Handelsgesellschaft* (1998) concerning the sale of designer eyeglass frames by Hartlauer, a discount chain with outlets in Austria that obtained the frames from an authorized dealer in Bulgaria, the ECJ decided that a trademark owner is entitled to prevent a third party not having his consent from using the trademark in relation to goods put on the market under that trademark outside the EEA and national rules could not provide for international exhaustion of trademark rights (Gould & Gribok, 1999). But complications arose because the trademark owner was able to prevent importation from outside the EEA only when it could be argued that the trademark owner had not consented to such importation.

The issue of consent became a crucial question that was addressed by the ECJ in its landmark ruling in *Zino Davidoff SA v. A & G Imports Ltd.; Levi Strauss & Co., Levi Strauss (UK) Ltd. v. Tesco Stores Ltd., Tesco plc, and Costco Wholesale U.K. Ltd.* (2001). The Tesco and Costco department store chains imported Levi's 501 jeans from North America and sold them in the U.K. at prices far lower than those offered by local authorized dealers. Levi Strauss filed trademark infringement suits against each company and the High Court of Justice of England and Wales that heard the two cases did not reject the retailers' argument that Levi Strauss had consented to the sale of the jeans because its contracts with the manufacturers in North America from whom the jeans were obtained did not explicitly prohibit export to Europe, but referred a series of questions including the issue of consent to the ECJ for resolution (Seidenberg, 2001). In a similar case where Zino Davidoff SA sued A & G Imports for importing "Davidoff Cool Water" perfume from Singapore into the U.K., the High Court of Justice of England and Wales inferred consent because the contract did not explicitly prohibit resale into Europe, but also sent the ECJ a series of questions on consent. The ECJ heard all three cases together (the German, French, Italian, Finnish and Swedish Governments, the Commission of the European Communities and EFTA Surveillance Authority also submitted observations to the Court) and ruled that the consent of a trademark owner to marketing within the EEA of products previously placed on the market outside the EEA must be unequivocal, whether express or implied, and such is not the case where the trademark owner is merely silent (European Court of Justice, 2001). While the decision effectively precludes unauthorized intermediaries from importing products from outside the EEA, parallel imports from within the EEA are still permissible. Companies like Tesco have indicated that they will continue to buy products like Levi's jeans from within the EEA for sale at discounted prices in the U.K. Gray market activity in the EEA will increasingly have to rely on products sourced from authorized dealers within the EEA.

CONCEPTUAL FRAMEWORK FOR UNDERSTANDING AND RESPONDING TO GRAY MARKET ACTIVITY

For qualitative research like the case study methodology employed here, the selection of cases largely depends on the conceptual framework developed from prior theory (Perry, 1998). Given the role theory plays in establishing appropriate research issues in case study research, we review the relevant literature on parallel channels of distribution and gray marketing. This literature review forms the basis of a theoretical framework for understanding and responding to gray market activity. Then, in the subsequent section, we present the case of Herman Miller v. ASAL GmbH which we use to explicate the theoretical model.

Causes of Gray Market Activity

Three causes of parallel marketing channels have been identified in the literature: (1) price differentials created by discriminating monopolists who set high prices in some market segments/countries; (2) exchange rate differentials; and (3) opportunistic behavior by members of administered marketing channels. Weigand (1991) suggests that these "Three factors, sometimes working alone but often in consort, virtually assure that parallel marketing channels will arise unless they can be stopped by trademark owners who seek to protect their authorized channel members.

Price Differentials
Most authors believe that price differences between markets are a necessary condition for the existence of gray markets (see for instance Cavusgil & Sikora, 1988; Cespedes, Corey & Rangun, 1988; Weigand, 1989). Absent price discrimination, little potential exists for gray marketing. However, when a product is available at different prices in two markets, there is an opportunity for an entrepreneur to buy the product in the market where prices are lower and sell it in the market where prices are higher. If barriers to arbitrage (e.g. trade restrictions, tariffs, transportation costs, regulations, etc.) do not preclude such activity, parallel channels of

distribution that are not authorized by the trademark owner will appear. When products are sold at different prices in different countries or at different prices to different market segments within a country (for a discussion of gray markets within the U.S., see Lowe & McCrohan, 1988), the potential for parallel channels of distribution exists. Innovations in communication and transportation such as the Internet and overnight air freight facilitate exploitation of these price differences and make the assumptions about market heterogeneity responsible for the price differences suspect.

Exchange Rate Differentials
Price differences may be the result of currency exchange rates (Duhan & Sheffet, 1988; Weigand, 1991). According to Bucklin (1989), gray marketing is a kind of arbitrage brought about by the inflexibility of pricing in response to exchange rate fluctuations. A differential exchange rate is likely to explain gray market transactions if the rate of change is swift (Weigand, 1991) and substantial. For example, suppose a product, ABC, was being manufactured in two countries, Argentina and the U.S., and the currency in Argentina devalued swiftly. Absent barriers to trade, a gray market could develop for ABC made in Argentina. If the firm making ABC continued to supply some countries/markets with ABC produced in the U.S. at the higher U.S. manufacturing price, entrepreneurs would attempt to buy ABC from a dealer or distributor in Argentina for less money and export it to those markets, including the U.S., where the cost/price is higher, thereby creating a parallel channel of distribution. Of course, the price differentiation caused by the exchange rate differential must be large enough to cover the costs of gray marketing including a reasonable profit.

When there is only one manufacturing location, swift and large changes in exchange rates could also create temporary arbitrage opportunities. If a country's currency drops in value, inventory imported before the decline may be priced low if the price is based on cost and the previous exchange rate. The parallel marketer would buy the product at the low price (i.e. with a stronger currency) and sell it in countries whose currency rose, until the pre-devaluation inventory is sold.

Opportunistic Behavior
Opportunistic behavior by middlemen, together with price differentials, also facilitates the creation of parallel channels in international markets. Such opportunistic behavior is likely to occur when the middleman's gross margin is disproportionately large relative to the marketing task performed and is particularly attractive if the transaction occurs outside the distributor's assigned territory. If the sale is geographically remote, the opportunistic distributor may assume

the sale is not made at the expense of the distributor's own full markup sales (Weigand, 1991).

The likelihood of opportunistic behavior and gray market activity is highest in international markets when conventional channels are employed. Perhaps for that reason, authorized channels in international markets are more likely to be administered, contractual or corporate channels, with the likelihood of opportunism and gray market activity being least for corporate channels. Nonetheless, as Weigand (1991) points out, opportunistic behavior by members of administered marketing channels may pay handsomely. A study of gray market activity affecting the export sales of U.S. manufacturing firms found that a greater degree of distribution control (price and physical distribution control), lower degree of channel integration, greater degree of centralization of management decision making, and greater degree of product standardization have a negative relationship with gray market activity (Myers, 1999). The study concluded that firms using commission agents and merchant distributors suffered most from gray market activity while joint venture partners, wholly-owned subsidiaries, and direct sale of exports to end users offered more control over the final sale of the product.

Outcomes of Gray Market Activity

Price differentials between markets, whether due to marketing strategy decisions or uncontrollable currency exchange rate fluctuations, provide the opportunity for arbitrage across markets and gray market activity. Clearly, there are winners and losers when gray market activity occurs. Parallel channel intermediaries, manufacturers, and buyers in certain industries benefit from gray market activity. Authorized channel intermediaries and manufacturers in some industries are hurt by gray market activity (unless they themselves initiate gray market activity).

Channel Intermediaries
Intermediaries who set up parallel channels of distribution discern an opportunity to benefit by selling at prices lower than those offered by the authorized channel and still make a profit. But intermediaries who are members of the authorized channel are hurt by gray market activity unless they themselves behave opportunistically and participate in gray market activity outside their assigned territory to maximize self-interest (e.g. to obtain bonuses or quantity discounts that would not be available based on sales solely within the assigned territory). Loss of sales due to lower priced gray market products causes conflict and leads authorized intermediaries to question the wisdom of their investment in requirements

mandated by the manufacturer (e.g. facilities and personnel to provide information and service to buyers before and after the sale, inventory of a full line of products). More often than not they will seek action from the manufacturer to cut off supply to unauthorized distributors.

Manufacturers

Manufacturers are hurt by the conflict with authorized channel intermediaries and the sales of products at reduced prices because of gray market activity. Efforts to improve the relationship with authorized intermediaries may include improved support in terms of cooperative advertising, improved factory warranties, etc. If parallel channels serve new market segments not served in the past by authorized channels, manufacturers benefit from their appearance. However, lack of control of unauthorized channels may have negative consequences, e.g. a failure to provide after-sales service by parallel channel intermediaries may harm the image of the manufacturer. Parallel channels may also foster intrabrand competition which may force authorized channels to do a better job serving their customers and lead to improved marketing strategies. It is conceivable that manufacturers may add gray marketers to the authorized channel or even acquire them, provided such actions do not lead to increased conflict with existing authorized intermediaries. In industries with high fixed costs where capacity utilization and economies of scale are important, manufacturers may require the incremental sales generated by parallel channels to sustain high production volumes. While parallel channels have a negative impact on authorized channels whose members include the manufacturers as well as intermediaries, the overall impact on manufacturers is less clear because of such benefits as access to new markets, improved marketing strategies, and production economies.

Buyers

The very existence of gray markets in which parallel channels meet the needs of buyers whose needs were not served or at least not served well indicates that buyers benefit from the appearance of parallel channels of distribution. Some buyers may have been unable to obtain the desired product because the authorized channel did not offer it in that market; other buyers may have been unwilling to pay a higher price for the product because it exceeded their reservation price; still others may not have needed the "bells and whistles" the authorized channel provided and wanted to pay a lower price for the basic product.

The appearance of unauthorized channels to meet the needs of buyers whose needs are either not served at all or are inadequately served may demonstrate the need for members of the authorized channel (manufacturers as well as distributors) to change their marketing practices and develop new marketing strategies and policies. An analysis by Bucklin (1993) suggests that gray markets are more a symbol of ineffective global marketing strategy than a barrier to such strategies.

Responses to Gray Market Activity

In recent years, increasing homogenization of international markets and the adoption of standardized marketing strategies globally have led to products with the same physical characteristics and brand name being sold worldwide. However, distribution strategies for these products have been limited by the channels available in these countries. Although the manufacturer may desire a standard set of service characteristics be provided as part of the product, variability in the provision of such services may be expected because many of these service characteristics are added by distributors. Prices of these products may also vary from country to country or region to region. Depending on local laws and customs the ability to control the price charged by the distributor is also likely to vary.

Pricing Strategy

Attempts to reduce gray market activity have to focus on reducing price differences by closely examining the basis for such differences and where appropriate, redefining markets and eliminating price discrimination. Prices in international markets may be coordinated by multinational companies to impede the appearance of parallel channels. Coordinated pricing permits local mangers to set prices but limits their discretionary control of the pricing decision. Four basic options for dealing with the interdependence of prices in different countries have been suggested: economic measures, centralization, formalization and informal coordination (Assmus & Wiese, 1995). Economic measures like transfer pricing, rationing, and specifying a price range may be used to coordinate prices at the country or regional level by a multinational company's headquarters (assuming centralized production outside the country and no violation of tax laws). Centralization attempts to prevent disparities in the optimal prices for each market resulting in gray market activity by instructing local managers to raise or lower prices. A compromise between the totally centralized and totally decentralized options, each of which has its pros and cons, is to apply similar pricing policies to all countries within a region. Formalization sets rules for local managers to follow in their pricing decisions, e.g. the price is set relative to a competitor's product or the price of the same product in another market. Informal coordination relies on common business values backed by compatible incentive systems to reduce opportunistic behavior. Even if a low price is optimal in a local market, the country manager would eschew the locally optimum price in order to prevent gray market activity and achieve optimal results for the firm as a whole.

Distribution Strategy

Efforts to curb gray market activity may include attempts by manufacturers to increase control of distribution decisions. Control is least in conventional channels of distribution where the intermediaries are independent merchants focused only on their own interests, higher in administered channels where the manufacturer or other member of the channel functions as a captain and attempts to ensure that channel members focus on the interests of the channel as a system, even higher in a contractual channel where the members enter into formal contracts that specify rights and responsibilities, and highest in corporate channels that are vertically integrated. But even if manufacturers establish corporate distribution channels and vertically integrate forward to sell directly to end users, the latter may still divert products to other customers or parallel channels of distribution. Cespedes, Corey and Rangan (1988) cite the example of a disk drive manufacturer who sold large quantities directly to original equipment manufacturers (OEMs) at a volume discount. Despite purchase agreements requiring the OEMs to add technical value to the product, they resold the raw product to computer dealers, systems houses, OEMs, and end users, forming a parallel channel of distribution. Unless vertical integration of distribution is accompanied by uniform pricing, parallel channels will still emerge.

Product Strategy

Much of the pressure on prices is a result of the standardized product being treated as a commodity that is easily transferred across markets. An obvious solution is to differentiate the product. The product is a bundle of physical, service and image characteristics and differentiation implies changing one or more of these characteristics to make it less substitutable and reduce cross elasticity across markets (Sashi & Stern, 1995). Product differentiation "can be a very effective method for stifling the gray market" by designing products with exclusive features that appeal to a particular market (Cavusgil & Sikora, 1988, p.81). Bundling the requisite physical, service and image characteristics for each market makes the product more appealing for that market and less desirable for other markets, reducing the potential for parallel channels of distribution.

The emphasis in product differentiation strategies is on tailoring the product to a particular market and obtaining the desired price by providing commensurate or greater value to the buyer. The reduced substitutability across markets and the concomitant reduction in potential for gray market activity is a consequence of the focus on satisfying buyer needs rather than the cause for product differentiation. Local needs for physical characteristics like labels in local languages, safety regulations and different ingredients result in product differentiation that may preclude gray market activity (Michael, 1998). A rather simplistic attempt at product differentiation designed to combat gray market activity is to limit warranty and after-sales service to products sold by authorized channels, the assumption being that parallel channel members are free riders who benefit from the value-adding functions provided by the authorized channel members. But in many cases, parallel channel members may add value by advertising, participating in trade shows, providing their own store warranty and service, etc. Although these activities significantly impact the nature of the product, they are outside the authorized channel's control. In fact, examination of the functions performed by parallel channels may reveal the needs of segments that have not been adequately served by authorized channels in the past, which represent an opportunity for the development of suitable product differentiation strategies by authorized channel members.

THE CASE OF HERMAN MILLER v. ASAL GmbH[3]

In early May 1999, Vreni Sahli, International Sales Manager for office furniture manufacturer Herman Miller, Inc. www.hermanmiller.com, received a call from John Paul Fournier, manager of Herman Miller Ltd.'s German operation. According to Ms. Sahli, Mr. Fournier "informed me that they had become aware of a company by the name of ASAL showing and selling chairs, Aeron chairs, in the German market." The Aeron chair, one of Herman Miller's most successful new product lines with "a patent list as long as your arm" www.hermanmillered.com/catalog/, is a unique, trademarked product nominated "Design of the Decade" by *Business Week* magazine. Mr. Fournier's concern stemmed from complaints from Herman Miller's authorized dealers/distributors who were surprised to find an established German firm, ASAL GmbH, selling Herman Miller Aeron chairs and keyboard trays at the INTERZUN International Trade Fair in Köln, Germany. Herman Miller had an established distribution system in Europe consisting of 100 or so authorized dealers/distributors with exclusive territories. ASAL GmbH was not one of them. Authorized Herman Miller dealers/distributors complained that ASAL GmbH was selling Aeron chairs for less money than they could buy them for! Keiro, a Herman Miller, Ltd. dealer in Europe called Herman Miller to ". . . say they have exclusive rights; (ASAL) can only sell chairs @ list price as per HMI."

Despite Herman Miller corporate policies which prohibit authorized dealers/distributors from selling directly to overseas clients outside their assigned territory, Mr. Fournier told Vreni Sahli that ASAL GmbH was acquiring the chairs through a Florida company. As International Sales Manager, Ms. Sahli reported directly to the VP of International Sales and Distribution. She did not typically get involved with exclusively U.S. dealers. However within days, she was on the phone with Jack Howard, General Manager of Herman Miller Florida, Inc. and President of Office Pavilion South Florida, Inc. Herman Miller Florida was Herman Miller's subsidiary in Florida and Office Pavilion South Florida was a company-owned dealer. "Jack did confirm for me that there was a document that had been signed by Office Pavilion in Miami with ASAL (Products Inc., a Florida corporation) with the intent to distribute keyboard trays for particular manufacturing environments in the German market through a company over there."

Vreni Sahli faced one of the toughest decisions of her seventeen year career at Herman Miller. By entering into a contract with Florida-based ASAL Products to sell Aeron chairs and keyboard trays for export to Germany, Herman Miller's subsidiary in Florida had created a parallel channel of distribution. What could or should she do about this "gray marketing" that was disrupting Herman Miller's authorized channels of distribution? She immediately called the Corporate Counsel, Jim Christiansen for advice.

Background Information

Herman Miller, Inc.
Herman Miller, Inc. is an office furniture manufacturer headquartered in Zeeland, Michigan. Their office furniture products include chairs, keyboard trays, desks, drafting tables, stools, etc. Herman Miller had sales of $1.7bn in 1998, $1.8bn in 1999 and $1.9bn in 2000. Table 1 provides three years of consolidated operating results for Herman Miller.

Herman Miller has an international distribution system comprised of "wholly-owned subsidiaries and they in turn, either sell on a direct basis or through distribution in specific geographies." Herman Miller's European subsidiary, Herman Miller Ltd., is headquartered in Bath, England. In 1999, Herman Miller Ltd. had contracts with about one-hundred distributors in Europe. In the U.S. market, Herman Miller also uses subsidiaries (e.g. Herman Miller Florida, Inc.) and company-owned distributorships (e.g. Office Pavilion South Florida, Inc.). In addition, there are independent distributors and dealers in Florida and elsewhere in the U.S. According to Ms. Sahli "A distributor is basically a retailer who covers a particular area from a sales standpoint and from a service standpoint. Very different from what we do as a corporation, which is at corporate level."

Table 1. Herman Miller (Consolidated Results)[a]
(from www.hermanmiller.com).

	2000	1999	1998
Operating results (in millions)			
Net sales	$1,938.0	$1,766.2	$1,718.6
Gross margin (3)	732.4	687.4	656.8
Selling, general, and administrative (3)	456.4	425.1	414.7
Design and research expense	41.3	38.0	33.8
Operating income	234.7	224.3	208.3
Income before income taxes	221.8	229.9	209.5
Net income	139.7	141.8	128.3
Cash flow from operating activities	202.1	205.6	268.7
Depreciation and amortization	77.1	62.1	50.7
Capital expenditures	135.7	103.4	73.6
Common stock repurchased plus cash dividends paid	$101.6	$179.7	$215.5
Key ratios			
Sales growth	9.7	2.8	14.9
Gross margin	37.8	38.9	38.2
Selling, general, and administrative	23.6	24.1	24.1
Design and research expense	2.1	2.1	2.0
Operating income	12.1	12.7	12.1
Net income growth (decline)	(1.5)	10.5	72.5
After-tax return on net sales	7.2	8.0	7.5
After-tax return on average assets	16.5	18.5	16.7
After-tax return on average equity	55.5	64.4	49.5

[a] For details, footnotes and other years, please see the Herman Miller web site.

ASAL GmbH and ASAL Products, Inc.

ASAL GmbH is a 60-year-old German firm in the office furniture business, among others. ASAL GmbH had more than 100 employees at three locations in the EU, and was owned 99% by its President, Mr. Barnard Stier. ASAL GmbH had sales of DM35.000.000 in 1996[4] and current sales of DM37.000.000.

In 1997, an ambitious young German named Oliver Asel took a job with an office furniture distributor, Herman Miller's Office Pavilion South Florida, Inc. At Office Pavilion he became knowledgeable about Herman Miller's line of office furniture including pricing for products such as the Aeron chair and keyboard trays.

In April 1998, Oliver Asel moved back to Germany to work for ASAL GmbH (no relation, herein after referred to as Oliver for simplicity) as Sales Manager. At that time, the EU was implementing new harmonized office health standards covering issues such as distance to the computer monitor and appropriate seating.

Oliver believed that Herman Miller keyboard trays combined with the Aeron chairs were an excellent solution to the new EU health standards. According to www.hmeurope.com, "the Aeron chair sets new standards for comfortable and health-promoting office seating...(it) meets and exceeds major international standards." Oliver convinced Mr. Stier that ASAL GmbH should pursue these product lines.

In September 1998, Oliver contacted Jean-Paul Fournier, German manager for Herman Miller Ltd. on behalf of ASAL GmbH. He was quoted DM229.5 for delivery of 1,000 keyboard trays. On September 30, 1998 the exchange rate was 1.6696 DM/$ so the quote was $137.46/tray. According to commercial web sites Aeron Chairs were being sold in the EU in small quantities for approximately DM1.800 to DM2.000 during May 1999. Using a May 12, 1999 *WSJ* exchange rate of 1.8359 DM/$, the prices were $960 to $1,200/chair.[5] However, based on his experience in Florida, Oliver knew that the same trays and chairs were being sold much cheaper in the U.S. Confronted with the Florida pricing information, Mr. Fournier told Oliver that if he did not like the prices in Germany, he should buy office furniture in America.

Oliver then contacted his former boss Gary Kemp, VP Operations at Office Pavilion South Florida to buy trays and chairs to sell in Germany. Because Herman Miller corporate policies forbid dealers/distributors from selling directly to overseas clients outside their assigned territory, Oliver was told that "if I wanted to buy keyboard trays from Herman Miller Office Pavilion, I have to form a U.S. company." As Jack Howard, the President of Herman Miller Florida and Office Pavilion explained, "If we were selling keyboard trays to ASAL U.S. or a Florida organization, that wouldn't be in violation of our (HM corporate) agreement."

In December 1998, Mr. Stier and Oliver formed a Florida Corporation, ASAL Products, Inc. for the purpose of re-exporting products purchased in the U.S. to ASAL GmbH in Germany. Mr. Stier owned 100% of the stock and the Board was the same as ASAL GmbH: Mr. Stier was President and Oliver was VP. The new firm was created as a "pass through" organization to circumvent the internal rules of Herman Miller, Inc.

Oliver negotiated a two-year purchase contract (January 8, 1999) with Gary Kemp, VP Office Pavilion for key board trays priced at $76.25 for quantities of less than 2,000 units. These were the same trays Mr. Fournier, the German manager for Herman Miller, quoted at the equivalent of $137.46/tray for orders of 1,000 or more, an 80% price differential. In an April 30, 1999 letter, a German Herman Miller dealer Norbert Stadler GmbH, quoted ASAL GmbH 1.970 DM/chair ($1,073.04) in quantities of 5–10 chairs and 1.760 DM/chair ($958.66) for 40–80 chairs. In May 1999, Office Pavilion South Florida agreed to sell ASAL Products an unlimited number of Aeron chairs at $511/chair (in lots of 2,000 or more) through the end of 2000, as well as a new model keyboard tray with palm rest and mouse tray at $173.24. The prices quoted by Norbert Stadler GmbH were more than 85% higher than the $511 price for nearly identical[6] Aeron chairs in Florida.

Under the contract and its addendums, Office Pavilion agreed to deliver keyboard trays and chairs to ASAL Products Inc. in Florida with the written understanding that ASAL Florida would export those products to ASAL Germany. A contract with a parallel structure was signed between ASAL Products, Inc. and ASAL GmbH to create the pass-through organization. Mr. Stier felt confident about his new Vice President Oliver Asel and the parallel channel of distribution they created to arbitrage the existing price differentials (see Fig. 1).

In 1999, Oliver returned to the U.S. and opened an office for ASAL Products in Fort Lauderdale, FL. Three or four small orders for trays and chairs were placed from ASAL GmbH through ASAL Products to Office Pavilion. The orders were paid for, shipped to ASAL Product, Inc.'s freight forwarder and exported to ASAL GmbH in Germany for resale. Everything transpired as agreed upon so ASAL GmbH, with Office Pavilion's knowledge, made arrangements to attend the INTERZUN, an international trade fair in Germany, to market these products.

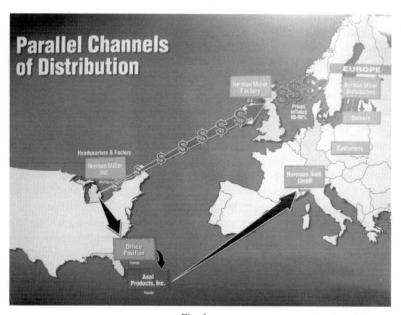

Fig. 1.

Oliver had already given Office Pavilion a short-term sales forecast of 5,000 to 7,000 Aeron chairs and thousands of keyboard trays. With the trade show coming up, Office Pavilion was abuzz. Everyone from warehouse workers to front office staff to top executives were discussing the large potential sales to Oliver and the big impact such sales could have on their bonuses. At Office Pavilion, sales people received commissions and the staff received EVA (Economic Value Added) bonuses based on year-end performance. Therefore, everyone at Office Pavilion had personal motivation to increase sales and profit.

INTERZUN INTERNATIONAL TRADE FAIR, KÖLN, GERMANY, MAY 7–11, 1999

International Trade Fairs are far more important in EU marketing in general and in Germany in particular. In preparation for the show, ASAL mailed letters and postcards to existing customers, as well as prospective new customers in Germany and throughout Europe. Office Pavilion employees expedited sample Aeron chairs and the new keyboard trays for exhibition at the INTERZUN. At the fair, ASAL had a good location and Oliver served as the technical representative. Their reception was much greater than expected. As Oliver said, "Chairs were flying out the door – unbelievable." He also noted that "I met some gentleman from Herman Miller International at the trade show."

Because of the importance of EU trade fairs, attendance is audited in a manner analogous to America's Nielsen ratings. The Audited Trade Fair and Exhibition Figures for the May 1999 INTERZUN (FKM, 2000 – see Table 2) showed audited numbers of 59,343 paid visitors. Eighty-three percent of those visitors were owners, directors, mangers or staff with decisive or collective responsibility for purchasing decisions. Although most were primarily small firms with less than five-hundred employees, 5,934 firms had five-hundred or more employees and there were 1,187 firms larger than 10,000 employees. Given the product market (chairs and keyboard trays), number of employees was a good proxy for potential demand.

On May 12, 1999, immediately after the INTERZUM trade show, ASAL GmbH sent a written forecast and orders to ASAL Products, Inc. for 32,320 Aeron chairs and 16,300 keyboard trays valued at over $21.8 million for delivery by September 1999. The same day, ASAL Products submitted their first order to Office Pavilion for 2,480 Aeron chairs, accompanied by a check for $633,840 (50% deposit). Office Pavilion VP of Operations, Gary Kemp and General Manager, Don Britton agreed to meet Oliver the next day to discuss/process the order. Table 3 shows the total projected sales volume of keyboard trays and Aeron chairs for the balance of ASAL Product Inc.'s two-year contract with Herman Miller's Office Pavilion.

Table 2. Audited Trade Fair & Exhibition Figures, Report 1999.

Total Number of visitors	**59,343**	**Position in the company/organization**	%
Proportion of trade visitors	98%	Entrepreneur, partner, self-employed	36
Region of Residence	%	Managing director, board members, head of an authority, etc.	18
Over 100 km away	86	Senior department head, other employee with managerial	
		responsibility	8
Total Germany	55	Department head, group head	12
Baden Wurttemberg	14	Other salaried staff	16
Bavaria	12	Skilled Worker	2
Berlin	1	Lecturer, teacher, scientific assistant	1
Brandenburg	—	Trainee, student	5
Bremen	1	Other	3
Hamburg	2		
Hesse	7	**Area of Responsibility**	%
Mecklenburg-West Pommerania	1	Management	48
Lower Saxony	5	Research/development/design	9
North Rhine-Westphalia	43	Planning/work preparation	6
Rhineland-Palatinate	7	Manufacture/production 13	
Saarland	2	Buying/procurement	9
Saxony	2	Administration/organization/personnel/social	
Saxony-Anhalt	1	welfare/training	2
Schleswig-Holstein	1	Marketing/sales/advertising/PR	9
Thuringia	1	Other	4
Total Foreign	**45**	**Frequency of visits to trade fair**	%
EU	59	1997	50
Rest of Europe	13	1995	36
Africa	3	1993	27
Central & South America	5	First Visit	42
North America	5		
Middle East	7	**Size of company/organization**	
East Asia	4	Number of employees %:	
Australia	4		

Number of employees %:

1- 9 30	200–499.......... 12
10–49 28	500- 999 4
50-99 11	1000- 9999............ 4
100-199 10	10 0000-and more ..2

Economic Sector	%
Industry	45
Skilled trades	25
Trade	20
Self-employed	6
Other	4

Length of Stay

1. Length of Stay (days) %:

one 57	four 5
two 21	five 5
three 12	

2. Average length of stay = 1.8days

3. Share of visitors on the event's days %:

1st day 30	4th day.......... 40
2nd day 39	5th day.......... 31
3rd day 40	

Influence on Purchasing/ procurement	
decisions	%
Decisively	56
Collectively	27
In an advisory capacity	10
No	7

Table 3. ASAL's Projected Sales Volume (No. of Units[a]).

	Keyboard Trays	Aeron Chairs
1999		
May	650	2,480
June	3,750	13,000
July	5,680	13,790
August	6,080	2,790
September	2,780	2,630
October	880	790
November	880	790
December	880	790
1999 sub-totals	21,580	37,060
2000		
January	880	790
February	880	790
March	880	790
April	880	790
May	880	2,820
June	3,880	12,790
July	4,880	11,290
August	4,880	2,790
September	1,780	2,630
October	880	790
November	880	790
December	880	790
2000 sub-totals	22,460	37,850

[a] Assumptions
1. The International Trade Show in Cologne will yield the same sales in 2000 as in 1999.
2. The management made large "house" sales of 8,500 chairs in June and July and will do so again in 2000.

ASAL's sales projections are based on the actual numbers sold by their sales force, management's prior "in-house" sales, and the outstanding results of the international trade fair. Tables 4 and 5 show proforma income statements for ASAL Products, Inc. and ASAL GmbH respectively based on those sales projections.

The very next day everything changed. Vreni Sahli became involved and decisions on what actions to take were elevated to corporate and the International Sales and Distribution division. Herman Miller found itself in a difficult predicament. ASAL Products, Inc. had a valid and operating contract to buy Aeron chairs and keyboard trays in the U.S. and export these products to Europe. Yet, there were authorized distributors and dealers in Europe with exclusive territories. Herman

Table 4.   ASAL Products, Inc. Proforma Income Statement.

	1999	2000	Total
Sales revenue			
Keyboard trays	$3,522,719	3,666,370	
Aeron chairs	21,914,319	22,381,462	
Total sales	25,437,038	26,047,832	51,484,871
Less cost of goods sold			
Keyboard trays	2,736,560	2,848,153	
Aeron chairs	18,937,660	19,341,350	
Cost of goods sold	21,674,220	22,189,503	43,863,722
Gross margin	3,762,819	3,858,330	7,621,148
Less operating expenses	91,373	266,434	–
Net profit	3,671,446	3,591,896	$7,263,341
Avg. sales price	DM$		
Keyboard trays	299.7	$163.24	
Aeron chairs	1,085.6	$591.32	
Fx rate	1.8359	DM/$	
	12-May-99	WSJ	

Miller, Inc. had to make a strategic decision quickly. Office Pavilion's General Manager, Donald Britton and VP Gary Kemp waited for a call from Jack Howard with directions from HQ.

DISCUSSION

Implications for Theory and Practice

Most authors agree that price differentials are the primary reason for the existence of gray markets (see for instance Cavusgil & Sikora, 1988; Cespedes, Corey & Rangun, 1988; Weigand, 1989). Data in the Herman Miller v. ASAL GmbH case attest to the potential for huge price differentials within Europe and support the theory that substantial price differences for nearly identical goods create an opportunity for entrepreneurs to arbitrage the differences.

Exchange rates supplied in the case allow us to evaluate exchange rate fluctuation as a potential explanation for price differentials. Although they had an assembly plant in England, Herman Miller manufactured its keyboard trays and Aeron chairs in the U.S. Since ASAL was acquiring these products in the

Table 5.   ASAL GmbH (HM Chairs & Trays Only) Proforma Income Statement.

	1999	2000	Totals
Sales revenue			
Keyboard trays	$5,110,836	5,319,248	
Aeron chairs	28,765,456	29,378,643	
Total HM product sales	33,876,292	34,697,891	68,574,183
Less cost of goods sold			
Key board trays	3,522,719	3,666,370	
Aeron chairs	21,914,319	22,381,462	
Cost of HM goods sold	25,437,038	26,047,832	51,484,871
Gross margin	8,439,253	8,650,059	17,089,312
Less operating expenses			
Sales commission, 2% of sales	677,526	693,958	
Six additional employees	114,333	228,667	
Overhead costs of added employees	16,736	33,471	
Marketing & International Trade Fair	13,617	103,611	
Warranty, ASAL GmbH 1.1%	372,639	381,677	
Freight, storage & handling 10%	2,543,704	2,604,783	–
Net profit	4,700,698	4,603,891	$9,304,589

country of manufacturing origin, the only foreign currency exchange rate that is relevant in this case is DM/$. The Deutsche Mark depreciated 11.6% against the dollar in the seven months from the end of September 1998 to the beginning of June 1999 (see Table 6). Therefore, Aeron inventory in Germany purchased before September 30, 1999 could be lower priced in Deutsche Marks relative to new purchases from the United States in May or June of 1999. However, if this were the cause of the price differentials, the gray market goods would flow in the opposite direction. Therefore, it is safe to rule out exchange rate fluctuations as the cause in this case.

Table 6.   DM/$ Exchange Rates.

Date	fx rate WSJ	Aeron's DM Cost (@$590)
September 30, 1998	1.6696 DM/$	985.06 DM
January 12, 1999	1.6909 DM/$	997.63 DM
May 12, 1999	1.8359 DM/$	1,083.18 DM
June 2, 1999	1.8882 DM/$	1,114.04 DM

Beside currency exchange rates, other underlying reasons for the existence of price differentials include demand differences and segmentation strategies (Duhan & Sheffet, 1988; Weigand, 1991). As Weigand (1991) points out, "The problem now more commonly derives from sellers whose strategy includes acting as discriminating monopolists and from opportunistic middleman who break their allegiance to the channel family."

Discriminating monopolists are those firms that set high prices in some market segments/countries. A firm like Herman Miller may choose to price low in one market (e.g. the U.S.) and high in another (e.g. Germany) because customers are more or less price sensitive (elasticity of demand) or because their profit maximizing business model calls for penetrating one market (the U.S.) to achieve economies of scale and skimming another (Germany) to increase overall profits.

Opportunistic behavior by middlemen, in conjunction with price differentials, is another potential cause of parallel channels in international markets. Gray marketing and parallel channels of distribution are in general legal (exceptions include Hong Kong and Taiwan), and the rights of gray marketers and those who create parallel channels of distribution are often protected by law. For instance, the European Commission has levied heavy fines against companies trying to limit gray market transactions within the EU. Volkswagen shoppers from Austria and Germany tried to buy Volkswagen cars in Italy where they were 30% cheaper. When VW ordered its Italian dealers not to sell cars to Europeans from outside Italy, they were fined $110 million by the EU Commission (*Financial Times*, 1998). In Todhunter-Mitchell & Co. Ltd. v. AnheuserBusch Inc. (1994), U.S. courts awarded treble damages to the parallel distributor from the multinational, AnheuserBusch, that interfered in the parallel distribution of Budweiser in the Bahamas (Michael, 1998). The case of Herman Miller v. ASAL GmbH demonstrates that where large price differentials continue to exist, international entrepreneurs will continue to find a way to create parallel channels of distribution, driving down consumer prices and making a legal profit.

It is also interesting to note that lack of transparency in pricing and measurements, currency conversion and carrying costs, and shopping and transportation costs, all between countries, have facilitated price differentials within the EU. However, England and Ireland recently converted from miles and pounds to kilometers and kilograms and twelve of fifteen EU countries now share a common currency, the euro. Such changes have made pricing and measures much more transparent. The Internet and the elimination of customs between member states have reduced shopping and transportation costs. We expect these changes and the economic forces set in motion will lead to lower price differentials within the expanded EU. The changing scenario has important implications for firms concerned with market entry strategies and international pricing and distribution channels. Price differences between European countries for products can be expected to converge over time, differenced at most by the transportation and transaction costs of parallel channels. An open question remains whether this harmonization of prices across the European market will be driven by the multinational corporations or their accomplices, the gray marketers and their parallel channels of distribution. The opportunities for entrepreneurs in Europe to arbitrage price differences within the EU and EA may improve with the increases in transparency and reduced costs of information and transportation. Nonetheless, if these economic forces cause the convergence of prices across the EEA as postulated, the opportunity may be a fleeting victory for independent international traders who create parallel channels of distribution.

The Importance of Trade Shows

The case also highlights the relative importance of International Trade Shows. Marketing goods and services through international trade fairs has been a European tradition for more than 1,200 years (Czinkota & Ronkainen, 1990). International trade fairs are far more important in international than domestic marketing (Cateora & Graham, 2002; Root, 1994). They are a special kind of market that brings buyers and sellers from many different countries together at one time and place. Unlike trade shows in the U.S. where a social or party atmosphere is common, trade fairs in Europe are an important part of the marketing mix to be prepared with great care (Onkvisit & Shaw, 1997). Cateora and Graham (2002) note that "European trade shows attract high-level decision makers who are not attending just to see the latest products but are there to buy. Europeans . . . focus on providing an environment for in-depth dealings." These paid visitors are in a buying mood and come to buy on the spot (Onkvisit & Shaw, 1997; Root, 1994). As such, the trade show or fair has become the primary vehicle for doing business in many foreign countries, serving as the most important vehicle for selling products.

The contract that Office Pavilion signed with ASAL Products explicitly planned for sales in Germany. Apparently the President of Herman Miller Florida, Jack Howard, and the managers of Office Pavilion, Don Britton and Gary Kemp, thought that the parallel distribution channel into Germany would not be visible or disruptive enough to draw the attention of Herman Miller Ltd. and headquarters in Michigan. Don Britton and Gary Kemp supported ASAL's participation in the INTERZUM without suspecting that it would cause such a commotion. However, as the audited figures show (see Table 2), 45% of the 59,343 paid visitors to this international trade show were from other countries in Europe and the rest of the world. For instance, 7% (i.e. 1,870) of the foreign attendees were from the Middle East and 62% of the foreigners (more than 16,500) were from other European countries. Apparently the Americans were caught off guard by the sales potential at an international trade fair, especially the sales to many firms outside Germany. The fact that Herman Miller dealers and distributors were at the INTERZUN and that sales were going to interfere with established channels in many countries magnified the problem, elevating it to the level of International Sales and Distribution at corporate headquarters. This case supports the literature that differentiates international trade shows, especially those in Europe, from trade shows in the U.S. These international trade fairs can serve as an important element in international market entry strategies. They can also wreak havoc with established channels of distribution if individual dealers or distributors sell products across the markets of other authorized intermediaries.

Limitations and Future Research

In evaluating research through the case method, it is clearly desirable to have more than one case study. However, it is very difficult to get firms to openly talk about their actions relative to gray markets or parallel channels of distribution because of strategic considerations and because of potential legal risks. Many of the issues and potential responses from a manufacturer's perspective raise price fixing and anti-trust concerns as the long history of litigation demonstrates. While this case study provides a basis for evaluating theory and practice, results and conclusions are obviously circumscribed by this limitation. Multiple in-depth case studies from different industries and nations would provide a richer texture for more reliable evaluation of theory and practice. Moreover, it may be advantageous to test this theory for statistical generalizability in future, more quantitative research studies (Perry, 1998).

CONCLUSION

Parallel channels of distribution and gray marketing can be a threat or an opportunity, depending on perspective. For multinational manufacturing firms, the threat to established distribution channels is clear. Nonetheless, the existence of parallel channels points to a marketing opportunity for the manufacturing firm's products that should be carefully considered. For the entrepreneurial international trader, price differentials between markets for nearly identical products create a profitable business opportunity. While there are some risks (e.g. potential service and warranty issues), consumers generally benefit from gray markets. This literature review and case study highlight each of these possibilities.

NOTES

1. The authors are not aware of any case studies but limited their search to a selection of current international business and international marketing textbooks.
2. This article and the embedded case study are available without cost to academics for inclusion in text books or for classroom discussion, merely by properly referencing *Advances in International Marketing*.
3. This case was developed as a basis for evaluating theory versus practice and to facilitate classroom discussion rather than to illustrate the effective or ineffective handling of an administrative situation.
4. On June 10, 1999, Jean-Paul Fournier received a report on the financial strength of ASAL GmbH. The D & B report showed that ASAL GmbH had 1996 sales of DM 35,000,000 or about $20 million dollars US. It also showed that the company financial resources were from 4 to 20 million DM (the basis is the total wealth) or between $2.2 million and $11.1 million dollars. Those sales and wealth numbers indicate that ASLA GmbH, while hardly a start-up company, was still very small relative to Herman Miller.
5. For instance, a price quote in April from Norman Stadler GmbH listed the chairs at DM1,970 for 5–10 units and DM1,760 in lots of 40–80 and Keiro's web site listed the Aeron chair at DM2,170 each. The exchange rate at that time was 1.8359 DM/$.
6. The only differences in the chairs were the numbering system and a slight difference (less than an inch) in the height adjustment.

ACKNOWLEDGMENT

The authors wish to thank Keith Grumer and Maidenly Sotuyo-Macaluso for their help with the facts of the case study and the reviewers for their helpful comments.

REFERENCES

Assmus, G., & Wiese, C. (1995). How to address the gray market threat using price coordination. *Sloan Management Review, 36*(3), 31–41.
Automotive News (2002). Kiss or kill it, March 4, *76*(5973), 12.
Ball, D. A., McCulloch, W. H., Frantz, P. L., Geringer, J. M., & Minor, M. S. (2002). *International business: The challenge of global competition* (8th ed.). Boston, MA: McGraw-Hill Irwin.
Bucklin, L. P. (1989). The gray market threat to international marketing strategies. Working paper. *ORSA/TIMS*, Marketing Science Conference.
Bucklin, L. P. (1993). Modeling the international gray market for public policy decisions. *International Journal of Research in Marketing, 10*, 387–405.

Cateora, P. R., & Graham, J. R. (2002). *International marketing* (11th ed.). Boston, MA: Irwin McGraw-Hill.

Cavusgil, S. T., & Sikora, E. (1988). How multinationals can counter gray market imports. *Columbia Journal of World Business, 23*(Winter), 75–85.

Cespedes, F. V., Corey, E. R., & Rangan, V. K. (1988). Gray markets: Causes and cures. *Harvard Business Review* (July–August), 75–82.

Chaudhry, P. E., & Walsh, M. G. (1995). Gray marketing of pharmaceuticals. *Journal of Health Care Marketing, 15*(1), 18–23.

Chen, H. L. (2002). Gray marketing and unfair competition. *Atlantic Economic Journal, 20*(June), 196–225.

Cross, J., Stephens, J., & Benjamin, R. E. (1990). Gray markets: A legal review and public policy perspective. *Journal of Public Policy and Marketing, 9*, 183–194.

Czinkota, M. R., Rivoli, P., & Ronkainen, I. A. (1992). *International business*. Fort Worth, TX: Dryden Press.

Czinkota, M. R., & Ronkainen, I. A. (1990). *International marketing* (2nd ed.). Chicago, IL: Dryden.

Daniels, J. D., & Radebaugh, L. H. (2001). *International business: Environments and operations* (9th ed.). Upper Saddle River, NJ: Prentice-Hall.

Duhan, D. F., & Sheffet, M. J. (1988). Gray markets and the legal status of parallel importation. *Journal of Marketing, 52*, 75–83.

European Commission (2002). Enlargement of the European Union: Candidate Countries in facts and figures (June).

European Court of Justice (2001). Judgment of the court in joined cases C-414/99 to C-416/99, accessed online at http://curia.eu.int/jurisp/cgi

Financial Times (1998). On the road to price convergence. November 12, 29, as reported in Kotabe and Helsen (2002).

FKM (2000). *Audited trade fair and exhibition figures, report 1999*. Society for voluntary control of fair and exhibition statistics (August).

Gould, L. F., Jr., & Gribok, S. P. (1999). Silhouette case shades parallel importation rules in Europe. *The Legal Intelligencer* (April).

Hill, C. W. L. (2001). *International business: Competing in the global marketplace: Postscript 2001* (3rd ed.). Boston, MA: Irwin/McGraw-Hill.

Johansson, J. K. (2003). *Global marketing: Foreign entry, local marketing and global management* (3rd ed.). Boston, MA: McGraw-Hill/Irwin.

Keegan, W. J. (2002). *Global marketing management* (7th ed.). Upper Saddle River, NJ: Prentice-Hall.

Keegan, W. J., & Green, M. C. (2003). *Global marketing* (3rd ed.). Upper Saddle River, NJ: Prentice-Hall.

Kiyak, T. (1997). International gray markets: A systematic analysis and research propositions. In: W. M. Pride & T. M. Hutt (Eds), *Proceeding of the American Marketing Association, Enhancing Knowledge Development in Marketing* (Vol. 8, pp. 92–93).

Kotabe, M., & Helsen, K. (2001). *Global marketing management* (2nd ed.). New York: John Wiley and Sons.

Kunert, P. (2002). Dealers and distributors at odds over grey markets. *MicroScope, 21*(26) (June 25), 12.

Levitt, T. (1983). The globalization of markets. *Harvard Business Review, 61*(3), 92–102.

Lowe, L. S., & McCrohan, K. (1988). Gray markets in the United States. *Journal of Consumer Marketing, 5*(Fall), 45–51.

Michael, J. (1998). A supplemental distribution channel? The case of U.S. parallel export channels. *Multinational Business Review* (Spring), 24–35.

Mullen, M. R. (1990). International channels of distribution: A review and analysis. In: H. Muhlbacher & C. Jochum (Eds), *Advanced Research in Marketing, Proceedings of the 19th Annual Conference of the European Marketing Academy* (Vol. 1, pp. 267–283).

Mullen, M. R., Tyler, K., Laffur, W., & Osland, G. (1999). International channels of distribution: Keys to entrepreneurial success: A review and analysis. In: A. Menon & A. Sharma (Eds), *Marketing Theory and Applications, Proceedings of the American Marketing Association Winter Educators' Conference* (Vol. 10, pp. 95–106).

Myers, M. B. (1999). Incidents of gray market activity among U.S. exporters: Occurrences, characteristics, and consequences. *Journal of International Business Studies, 30*(First Quarter), 10–126.

Onkvisit, S., & Shaw, J. J. (1997). *International marketing: Analysis and strategy* (3rd ed.). Columbus, OH: Merrill Publishing Company.

Perry, C. (1998). Processes of a case study methodology for postgraduate research in marketing. *European Journal of Marketing, 32*(9/10), 785–802.

Punnett, B. J., & Ricks, D. A. (1992). *International business*. Boston, MA: PWSKent Publishing Company.

Root, F. R. (1994). *Entry strategies for international markets*. New York, NY: Lexington Books.

Sashi, C. M., & Stern, L. W. (1995). Product differentiation and market performance in producer goods industries. *Journal of Business Research, 33*(June), 115–127.

Seidenberg, S. (2001). Levi's blues. *IP Worldwide* (July 24).

Sharma, D. C. (2002). Global economic slowdown not effecting handset sales in Asia-Pacific region. *RCR Wireless News* (April 22), (21/16), 28.

Todhunter-Mitchell & Co. Ltd. v. AnheuserBusch Inc., 375 F. Supp. 610 (E. D. Penn, 1974). modified 383 F. Supp. 586 (E. D. Penn, 1974).

Weigand, R. E. (1989). The gray market comes to Japan. *Columbia Journal of World Business* (Fall), 18–24.

Weigand, R. E. (1991). Parallel import channels – options for preserving territorial integrity. *Columbia Journal of World Business* (Spring), 53–60.

APPENDIX

Notes for Teaching

Herman Miller's Office Pavilion South Florida refused to fill ASAL Product's order for Aeron chairs after the INTERZUM. That action immediately cut off the supply of Aeron chairs for ASAL Products and, accordingly, ASAL GmbH.

Mr. Howard had advised Mr. Kemp and Mr. Britton to hold the order placed by ASAL and to try to put a meeting together. On June 7, 1999, Verni Sahli, John Paul Fournier, Jack Howard, Mr. Stier, Oliver Asel and Atilla Babacan met in Chicago to try to reach an agreement between Herman Miller International and ASAL Products, Inc. and ASAL GmbH. ASAL offered to sell most of the rights to the contract to Herman Miller for $5 million, while retaining some business for ASAL GmbH, or to make an outright sale of all of ASAL's rights under the contract for $10 million, including a list of those customers who had ordered the chairs. At the end of the meeting the parties agreed to think things over.

Subsequently, John Paul Fournier received the D&B report referred to in the case disclosing the relatively small size and financial strength of ASAL GmbH compared to Herman Miller. No further progress was made in discussions between the firms.

ASAL Products Inc., the Florida Corporation, filed a lawsuit v. Office Pavilion South Florida Inc. d/b/a Herman Miller Office Pavilion in the Circuit Court of the 17th Judicial Circuit in and for Broward County, Florida (Case # 99–0121132, Cace 13). The case was tried before a jury that awarded ASAL Products Inc. about $5million in damages, interest and costs. However, as of the date of this writing, the case is still under appeal awaiting final determination.

ASAL GmbH, the German firm, filed a lawsuit v. Herman Miller, Inc. and Office Pavilion South Florida, Inc. in the U.S. District Court in Broward County, Florida (Case No. 00–6986-CIV-DIMITROULEAS). The jury found Herman Miller, Inc. responsible for breach of contract but awarded no damages. However, as of the date of this writing, the case is still under appeal awaiting final determination.

Professor Michael Mullen www.drmullen.com acted as an expert witness in this case for the law firm of Grumer and Levin, P. A., Fort Lauderdale, Florida that represented ASAL Products, Inc. and ASAL GmbH. For a current update on this case, please check the legal references or e-mail the first author at mullen@fau.edu

PATENT ISSUES IN CHINA: ENTRY DECISIONS IN A DYNAMIC LEGAL AND COMPETITIVE ENVIRONMENT

Steven W. Kopp and Ka Zeng

ABSTRACT

The People's Republic of China has long craved advanced technologies, and has undertaken an overwhelming number of changes in its intellectual property laws in order to foster domestic innovation and to encourage foreign investment. China implemented its first patent law in 1985. However, implementation and enforcement of this law and its amendments have been difficult, such that many foreign firms are reluctant to invest in Chinese markets. This paper describes the many changes that have been made to Chinese patent laws, and then illustrates patent activity in China as those changes have been implemented. Managerial issues are discussed in detail.

INTRODUCTION

Intellectual property has become a new form of currency in world trade. At the national level as well as at the firm level, it is vital to control intellectual property on technology and production processes. For both developed and developing economies, IP protection has become a major negotiation point in cross-boundary trade.

At the same time, empirical research has provided strong evidence that a firm's patent activity is related to the future value of that firm (Deng, Lev & Narin, 1999).

Reviving Traditions in Research on International Market Entry
Advances in International Marketing, Volume 14, 107–124
© 2003 Published by Elsevier Science Ltd.
ISSN: 1474-7979/doi:10.1016/S1474-7979(03)14006-9

Companies in certain industries perform better in economic terms if they are patent-active (Ernst, 1995), as profitability and sales increase as patent portfolios increase in size (Narin, Noma & Perry, 1987). This positive relationship appears to hold across countries (Bloom & Van Reenen, 2002; Ernst, 2001; Hall & Bagchi-Sen, 2002). Additional studies have suggested that strong commitment to technology transfer can lead to superior subsidiary performance in the local market (Isobe, Makino & Montgomery, 2000). In a number of industries, it behooves a firm not only to defend its patents as valuable assets but also to consider them proactively as components of strategic market entry decisions.

China has long attached great importance to acquiring foreign technology to improve its stature in the world economy (China's New Trademark Policy . . . 1979; Kraar, 1985; Yu, 2000). But because China has had a reputation as a sanctuary for intellectual property piracy of all forms, foreign firms have been reticent to invest in the Chinese market. Thus, despite the government's professed desire to liberalize and globalize the Chinese economy, the risk of the loss of proprietary control has made it difficult for China to obtain foreign intellectual investment and know-how, particularly in industries in which innovation is central to survival.

The purpose of this paper is to describe and discuss the creation and changes of the patent system in China and then to examine the effects of these changes and the competitive environment that they create on entry strategies into the world's most populous market. The discussion first focuses on the enormity of the changes in China's patent laws that have been necessary for the country to gain access to the World Trade Organization. In seeking integration into the global marketplace, China has undertaken a series of legislative initiatives that brought the country's patent laws more in line with international standards. Then we examine the current business legal environment in China, with specific focus on the patent laws that are currently in effect, and discuss in detail the changes in patent activity since the institution of the new patent laws. While continuous efforts have been made to improve the protection of innovation, enforcement and litigation continue to be unpredictable. Finally, with this legal and competitive environment in mind, managerial recommendations with specific application to entry decisions into Chinese markets are provided.

THE ROAD FROM PERDITION: CREATION OF CHINA'S PATENT LAWS

While intellectual property laws have been in place in China for many years, it was only in the last two decades that a relatively comprehensive framework for patent protection has been established. Between the 1950s and early 1980s, the state served as the owner and ultimate arbiter of patent and other types of intellectual property. When an invention was found to be useful by the government, the inventing party would only be issued an inventor's certificate and a cash award, and would have to cede ownership of the patent to the state (Moga, 2001). This primitive, pre-patent-law form of protection was clearly inadequate from the point of view of China's Western trading partners such as the United States. During the 1980s, China's desire to become a world power compelled the country to seek integration into the global economy and admission to the General Agreement on Tariffs and Trade (GATT), now the World Trade Organization (WTO). The GATT/WTO acceptance process was then the mechanism that led to China's first national patent law. The GATT and the Agreement on Trade Related Aspects of Intellectual Property Rights (TRIPs) established comprehensive standards for the protection of intellectual property and the enforcement of intellectual property rights in WTO countries.

Table 1 provides the significant elements of China's first Patent Law and its subsequent amendments. In 1985, in order to address international concerns about patent protection so as to attract foreign investment and to facilitate the country's integration into the world economy, China adopted its first patent law.

The new law protected inventions, utility models, and designs based on the degree to which the innovation met the standards of novelty, inventiveness, and usefulness, largely conforming to the standard patent parameters for a developing country at the time.

The 1985 Patent Law represented an important stride in patent protection, but the conflict between the introduction of a form of private property and the deeply entrenched principle of socialist ownership resulted in implicit limitations on the granting of a variety of patent rights for which the law presumably offered protection. For example, the law concerned the privileges that entities, instead of individuals, enjoyed in applications for patents in service invention-creations, which referred to inventions and creations undertaken on or in relation to one's job or by using material or data from one's work unit (*danwei*). Given the centrality of *danwei* in China's socio-economic life in the mid-1980s, and the subsequent difficulty individuals faced in obtaining the necessary equipment and capital independent of one's *danwei*, this rule in effect precluded individual Chinese nationals from obtaining invention patents on their own. The law's specifications presented hurdles for Chinese nationals seeking patent protection because of its preference toward foreign applicants, its provisions on compulsory licensing, and its exclusion of broad groups of products. Indeed, the patent law seemed to have granted greater legal privileges to foreigners and their local partners than to other Chinese, presumably out of a desire to facilitate the transfer of advanced technology to China. Even with such a groundbreaking effort in the country's

Table 1.   Overview of China's Patent Law and Amendments.

	1985 Patent Law	1993 Amendment	2000 Amendment
Patentable subject matters	Prohibited patenting of chemicals, pharmaceuticals, and products obtained through chemical process	Removed these prohibitions	
Duration of protection	Provided 15 years of protection for invention patents; 5 years for utility models and designs	Provided 20 years of protection for invention patents; 10 years for utility models and designs	
Compulsory licensing	Granted governments at various levels with broad authority to license patents that are of great significance to the public interest	Restricted the grounds for the granting of compulsory license to two situations: (a) where an entity qualified to utilize the invention or utility model made a request to utilize the patent on reasonable terms; (b) where a national emergency or the public interests requires it	More specifically defined the relative value and subject matter of a patent for which a compulsory license would be granted
Protection of process patents	No provision	Extended patent protection to the product directly obtained by the patented process	
Offering for sale		No provision for patent owners to exclude third parties from offering for sale the patented products	Provided patent owners with the right to prohibit unauthorized "offering for sale"
Other			Burden of proof of infringement of process to the defendant; criteria for determining statutory damages

first patent law, the 1985 patent law also suffered from inadequate legal remedies. In part, to alleviate considerable trade pressure from the United States, China revised the original patent law for the first time in 1993.

The 1993 amendment removed the earlier restrictions against chemical, food, and pharmaceutical products, extended the duration of protection for a patent right, lifted certain limitations on the granting of rights (such as those associated with the granting of process patents), and imposed stricter standards on compulsory licensing. These changes brought China's patent regime more in line with the TRIPS requirements. Further, procedural changes shortened the amount of time for patent approval by an average time period of three to four months. These improvements aside, several provisions of the revised Patent Law still did not comply with the TRIPS Agreement. These issues were the focus of the second amendment to China's Patent Law, which was enacted in 2000. The 2000 amendment eliminated some of the major differences between the previous versions of the Chinese Patent Law and the TRIPS agreement. These administrative protections pertained to offering for sale, innocent infringement, preliminary injunction, and compulsory license. In addition, patentee friendly standards have been added to the determination of statutory damages and employment patent. Further, under the initial Patent Law, applicants often waited months or even years to find out whether the patent office has approved their applications.

In November 2001, China was granted WTO membership, but the country continues to modify its IP system. The State Intellectual Property Office began to accept foreign applications for registration of layout design of integrated circuits in December, 2001, and SIPO also signed a cooperation framework protocol with the World Intellectual Property Organization in May 2002, giving priority to the protection of copyright and patents, especially in the areas of e-commerce, domain names, and the protection of the rights of small and medium-sized companies.

THE LEGAL ENVIRONMENT

The legal system in China is dominated by criminal law with an elementary civil code that has been in effect since 1987. Foreign entities have the same legal rights and obligations as Chinese entities. Foreign entities wishing to bring an action in China must have a vital interest in the case, and those wishing to use an attorney must engage a Chinese attorney. In general business law, China has introduced numerous laws and regulations that deal with the commercial activities of foreigners. However, extensive interpretations are often still in the hands of local officials, and these interpretations can vary widely depending on the local official (Sanyal & Guvenli, 2001; Yu, 1991), so that, even with the changes enacted toward protection of patents, enforcement has been meager even in the recent past. Because of this, good connections with government officials are vital for businesses choosing entry modes as well as venture partners (Tse, Pan & Au, 1997).

Patent Law Environment

China enacted its Patent Law on April 1, 1985. During the three years prior to the enactment, many Chinese engineers and experts were sent to the West German Patent Office and to the Japanese Patent Office to be trained or to do research. Consequently, the foundations of the Chinese system are technically similar to those of Germany.

Chinese courts are divided into four levels: the Supreme People's Court, the Provincial Higher People's Courts (the level of provinces, municipalities under direct administration of central government, and autonomous regions), the Intermediate People's Courts (the level of cities and areas), and the District or County Courts. The Supreme People's Court has assigned forty-three of the four-hundred Intermediate People's Courts to serve as courts of first instance for patent infringement cases, with the corresponding higher level courts responsible for handling appeals. The Basic Courts hear first instance cases of intellectual property infringement other than patent cases.

There are seven categories of patent cases that are adjudicated by the Chinese People's Court:

• Disputes as to whether patent rights shall be granted.
• Disputes over patent validity.
• Disputes over compulsory licenses.
• Disputes over royalties to be paid for a compulsory license for a patent that has been granted.
• Disputes over royalties to be paid for a compulsory license that has been granted but has yet to be published.
• Disputes over patent infringement.
• Disputes as to the conclusion of contracts concerning the transfer of patent application rights or patent rights.

In intellectual property infringement cases, the domicile of the defendant or the place where the infringement activities took place determines which court has jurisdiction. In litigation involving important foreign intellectual property cases, the Intermediate Courts serve as courts of first instance, again with the corresponding higher-level court serving as appellate courts. In the civil system, parties have the right to appeal a decision made by the court of first instance; however, decisions of the appellate court are final and cannot be appealed.

Since 1985, China has maintained a dual system for handling patent infringement dispute under which the patentee may either request the Administrative Authority for Patent Affairs (AAPA) to handle the dispute or directly institute legal proceedings in court. An Administrative Authority exists in every province, autonomous region, and municipality. These authorities have the power to order an infringer to stop the infringement and to compensate the patent owner for the damage. Any party who is dissatisfied with the decision of the authority may institute legal proceedings in court. If such proceedings are not instituted within the time limit and if the order is not complied with, the authority may approach the court for compulsory execution. In addition to patent infringement cases, the authorities are also responsible for handling the passing off patent cases. Passing off essentially refers to counterfeiting of patented products, or manufacturing or selling non-patented products that are represented as being patented. Although recent efforts aimed at strengthening enforcement have more clearly defined the responsibilities of the relevant administrative agencies, they have largely left the dual system for handling patent infringement intact. So, even though Chinese courts appear to have wide jurisdictions, their power has nevertheless been undermined by the dual system for handling patent infringement disputes.

If a patent is used without the authorization of the patent holder, the patent holder has the right to request either that the administrative authority handle the matter or that the People's Court institute proceedings. If the patentee chooses to pursue the issue through administrative proceedings, the patentee has the right to appeal the decision to the Court within three months after notification of the administrative decision. The administrative authority has the authority and power to order the infringer to stop the infringing act and/or to compensate the patentee for damages.

China is also a signatory to the Patent Cooperation Treaty (PCT), which is a mechanism in place for promoting global patent harmonization. The PCT is administered by the World Intellectual Property Organization (WIPO). The PCT process allows companies to file one international patent application and simultaneously seek patent protection in the ninety-four signatory countries of the PCT. That application can be filed with a national patent office or with the International Bureau of the WIPO.

Specifics of the Patent Law and Its Amendments

There are three requirements for a patent:

Novelty: before the date of filing, no identical invention or utility model has been publicly disclosed in publications in China or abroad and that the model has not been publicly used or made known to the public by any means in China.

Inventiveness: compared with a technology existing before the date of filing, the invention has prominent substantive features and represents notable progress, and that a utility model has substantive features that represent progress.

Practical applicability: an invention or utility can be made or used, and can produce effective results.

In China, there are three types of patents: invention patents, utility patents, and design patents. Invention patents have a term of twenty years from the filing date of the patent application. Chinese invention patents correspond to what American patent practitioners would consider utility patents, and include as subject matter processes, machines, or compositions of matter. Both utility model and design patents have a term of ten years. Utility models more or less correspond to U.S. improvement patents, while design patents are roughly equivalent in both countries.

Invention patent applicants must pass two examination processes. The first examination is called the process examination and the second is called the substantial examination. In the process examination, the examiner only considers the contents of the process requirements such as the quantity and type of documentation, etc. In the substantial examination, however, the examiner analyzes the innovation, creativity and use of the patented item. Only invention patent applications are substantively examined under China's patent law. This examination process usually takes two to three years to complete before an invention patent is granted.

The utility model concept is a direct derivative of the patent system of Germany. A utility model is a tangible product or a new technological solution with practical application and a certain degree of novelty and inventiveness. Both inventions and utility models can be considered as technological solutions. However, there are some differences between the two. Utility patents only apply to new, practical technological solutions concerning the shape or structure of a product, whereas inventions must relate to the invention of a product or method. Also, the requirements for utility patents are less stringent than those for inventions. As long as a product has substantive features and improvement, an innovation can qualify for a utility patent. Because of this, the application procedures for utility models are relatively simple and do not require the second substantial examination. Thus, the time it takes for a utility model application to its granting is relatively short – between six months and one year. Finally, the design patent is the easiest to obtain, since it is based solely upon establishing some difference in the patented item's shape, color, etc. Receiving this type of patent usually takes about four to eight months.

Two further significant distinctions should be pointed out between the Chinese patent law and that of the United States. First, China has a first-to-file system of patent ownership, as opposed to America's first-to-invent system. So long as no other person has previously filed an identical application with the Patent Office published after the said date of filing, the application will be considered first-filed. Second, unlike American patent law, in which the inventor initially owns all rights irrespective of the type of invention, China's patent law distinguishes between service and non-service inventions. A service invention is one made by an inventor in execution of tasks basically in the course of the inventor's job, or made by the inventor mainly using the material and technical means of the employer. Patent rights for service inventions belong to the employer. Conversely, patent rights for non-service inventions vest in the inventor.

Patent Activity in China

Foreign and Domestic Patent Activity

Figure 1 provides a graphic representation of the total number of patent applications filed by Chinese domestic and foreign applicants since the inception of the Patent Law. Both domestic and foreign patent applications steadily increased between 1985 and 2000, although the percentage increase in domestic applications is significantly higher than that for foreign applications: from 1985 to 1999, the total number of domestic applications increased almost 15 times, from 9,411 to 140,339, whereas total foreign applications increased only six times, from 4,961 to 30,343.

Table 2 provides the total number of patent applications received by the China Patent Office, cumulatively reaching over one million applications by 2000. Patent applications increased by an annual average rate of 15.4% from 1995 to 1999.

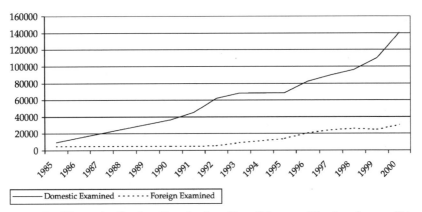

Fig. 1. Total Patent Applications Examined per Year, Chinese and Foreign. *Source: China Intellectual Property Statistical Yearbook* (2000).

Table 2. Percentage of Patent Applications Handled by the China Patent Office
(1985–2000).

Year	Total	Chinese Nationals (1995–2000)	Foreign Nationals (1995–2000)
Total	1166427	80.8	19.2
1985–1994	439529	87.3	12.7
1995	83045	83.7	16.3
1996	102735	80.8	19.2
1997	114208	78.9	21.1
1998	121989	78.9	21.1
1999	134239	81.9	18.1
2000	170682	82.2	17.8

Source: China Intellectual Property Statistical Yearbook (2000).

Figure 2 provides a graphic representation of the total number of patents granted
to Chinese domestic and foreign applicants since the inception of the Patent Law.
Again, the number of patents awarded to both domestic and foreign applicants
steadily increased between 1985 and 2000.

Between 1985 and 2000, the total number of patents approved by the patent
office reached 636,378 (see Table 3). Between 1995 and 1999, the number of
patent approvals increased by an annual average rate of 24.5%, but a 47.5% increase
from 1998 to 1999. Over the five-year period, the number of patents granted for
Chinese domestic applicants increased 30.0% per year, while the increase for
foreign applicants was 38.3%.

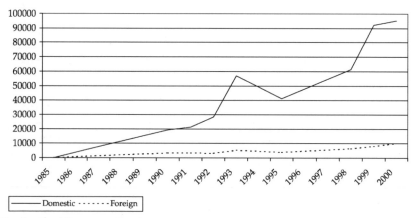

Fig. 2. Total Patent Applications Granted per Year, Chinese and Foreign. *Source: China
Intellectual Property Statistical Yearbook* (2000).

Table 3. Percentages of Patents Approved (1985–2000).

Year	Total	Chinese Nationals (1995–2000)	Foreign Nationals (1995–2000)
Total	636378	91.3	8.7
1985–1994	223152	91.2	8.8
1995	45064	92.9	7.1
1996	43780	92.1	7.9
1997	50992	91.0	9.0
1998	67889	90.4	9.6
1999	100156	92.0	8.0
2000	105345	90.4	9.6

Source: China Intellectual Property Statistical Yearbook (2000).

In terms of foreign patent applications by origin, the ten leading countries ranked according to patent applications filed with the Chinese Patent Office in 2000 are Taiwan, Japan, the United States, Germany, South Korea, Hong Kong, France, the Netherlands, Switzerland, and Great Britain (see Table 4). These countries are also those with the most investment in China.

Activity Across Patent Categories

The progressive development of the patent law regime in China has brought about increased patent applications. Between 1985 and 2000, the total number of applications for the three types of patents increased more than nine times, from 14,372 to 170,628. Applications for utility models consistently outpaced those for designs and inventions. In 2000, applications for utility models reached 68,815

Table 4. Foreign Country Patent Applications, 2000.

	Number of Patent Applications Examined	Number of Patent Applications Approved
Taiwan	10778	8465
Japan	9888	3594
United States	8418	2332
Germany	2787	871
South Korea	1861	608
Hong Kong	1374	1285
France	1387	537
Holland	993	311
Switzerland	867	408
UK	802	304

Source: China Intellectual Property Statistical Yearbook (2000).

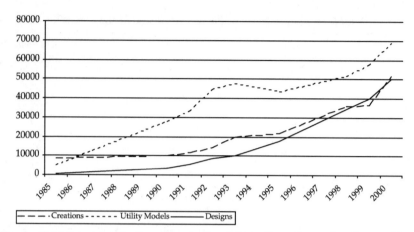

Fig. 3. Total Patent Applications Examined each Year, Three Categories. *Source: China Intellectual Property Statistical Yearbook* (2000).

(40.3%), compared to 50,120 for designs (29.4%) and 51,747 for inventions (30.3%) in that same year. Figures 3 and 4 present the trends in the three types of patent applications (e.g. inventions, utility models, and designs) examined and granted for the years 1985 through 2000. Applications for all three types of patents increased steadily during this period. The number of utility model applications examined and granted by the Patent Office experienced a relatively sharp increase in 1993, probably due in part to both the accession of China to

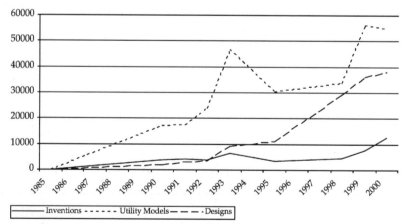

Fig. 4. Total Patent Applications Granted each Year, Three Categories. *Source: China Intellectual Property Statistical Yearbook* (2000).

the Patent Cooperation Treaty (PCT) and the amendments to the Patent Law that doubled the term of both utility models and design patents.

The next section will incorporate the preceding descriptions into a discussion of strategic and other managerial considerations.

DISCUSSION AND MANAGERIAL IMPLICATIONS

Success in the PRC often depends on a certain degree of adaptation to Chinese conditions and practices (Yang, Farley & Hoenig, 1999). In the present context, this adaptation should take into consideration specific aspects of the Chinese legal and patent systems, as well as the specific aspects of the firm's overall strategy and how its patents and other intellectual properties fit into its decision making. Much of what a firm must include in its entry decision is simply forward thinking. But more specifically, the management and protection of a firm's intellectual property should be a key portion of the firm's overall entry strategy.

Pre-entry Decisions

Strategic entry decisions may consist of a spectrum from the decision not to attempt entry into the market at all, to full-fledged wholly-owned subsidiary. In any decision to enter the Chinese market with patent-worthy products, some would argue to bring adequate, rather than the highest-tech into the market, to avoid the risk of losing the most current technologies to competitors. For example, the Boeing Corporation routinely gives away older technologies that are in danger of being copied, thus eliminating the returns to copying, and essentially leapfrogging its own technology availability.

It is also desirable to gain patent protection prior to introducing any product or establishing any distribution of a product. Because China is a first-to-file patent system, even though use of a product may take place in another country preceding Chinese introduction, a patent application may be filed by someone other than the original patent owner. For example, before choosing a location for a plant in mainland China, the Taiwan Semiconductor Manufacturing Company chose first to register over 3,000 of its patents there.

In terms of selecting joint venture or other partners in the distribution of a patentable product, care should be taken to select a collaborator who is unlikely to steal and has the clout to deter those who would infringe. In 1989, the Koller Group, a manufacturer of industrial products, determined that one of its patented products, a spring used as a component in video cassettes, was being pirated by one of its customers. Although the infringing customer was caught red-handed, the bureaucracy of the patent administration office proved to be the greater hurdle, and the case was finally decided in Koller's favor after nine years (How U.S. firm . . . 1997).

Entry Mode Decisions

Essentially, the more directly involved a firm is in its Chinese venture, the greater the firm's ability to protect its intellectual property. As mentioned earlier, much of China's patent protection regime is designed to encourage smaller and medium-sized firms to develop new technologies. Technology-based start-up firms face a complex and highly strategic trade-off, because the choice of foreign sales mode may have profound implications for patent protection. Those firms who engage Chinese markets as export-only will find it more difficult to police and protect their technological products than some type of direct capital investment such as a wholly-owned foreign subsidiary.

Research on smaller firms in the high-tech arenas suggests that entry modes are characterized by relatively low resource commitment and are directed more toward commercialization rather than foreign production. However, the research also offers that technology-based start-ups have a propensity to enter several foreign markets within a short time span (Burgel & Murray, 2000). If China is included among those markets, the entering firm should consider registering its patents under Patent Cooperation Treaty (PCT) status. Because China is a signatory to the treaty, an application for a patent in any other PCT signatory nation can be activated in China. PCT registrations are more paper intensive and not all patent offices trust the search results. The benefit, however, is that it makes it much easier to file in multiple jurisdictions, eases the front-end filing process and lowers the cost of filing since there is only one filing fee, even if the application is subsequently adapted to fit national or regional requirements. PCT registration also prevents competitors from filing substantially the same patent in other countries after the initial patent is issued.

The choice of entry mode may be dictated by the maturity of the firm. That is, even for firms that produce patentable, specialized products, direct exporting may not be an appropriate choice for start-up firms (Zacharakis, 1997), hence the necessity of selecting an export agent or other distributor. For patented materials, the patent owner should license the patent to the distributor.

Licensing and Contractual Decisions

Companies wishing to license their patent rights should include several significant contractual provisions in their Chinese licensing agreements. First, the agreement should specify a choice-of-law provision, which will establish the court of jurisdiction for any contractual disputes thereafter. It is extremely costly, in time and expense, for a foreign licensor to pursue a licensee for lost revenue. Second, the licensing agreement should designate an authorized representative to receive any service of process for breaches of the licensing agreement. In other words, the parties should decide and agree in advance on a legitimate agent – a lawyer, for example – to whom any summons or other notice could be served. Third, the licensing agreement should mandate that the licensee will require all sublicensees to be bound by the terms of the initial licensing agreement, and to subject sublicensees to the same jurisdiction. It should also be specified in any licensing agreement whether the technology transferred is transferred to the licensee. In other words, the licensee is to be held strictly liable for any harm that results to the licensor when a sublicensee fails to adhere to the original license, and the use of the patented technology is clearly outlined prior to any use on the part of the licensee. This provides the licensee with considerable incentive to protect the licensed patent's rights.

Additionally, within the domain of a firm's human resource management contracts, it is important to have all employees, including local partners, managers, and workers, sign and understand a general non-disclosure agreement. Training for local staff as to what comprises intellectual property – patented materials and trade secrets especially – how it benefits the company and the worker, and how its protection may appeal to and draw more innovation-driven firms to China and further develop China's own technology industries. In terms of the dissemination of technical knowledge, it may be recommended that vital knowledge about patents and processes are centralized or dispersed in such a way that each employee has incomplete information, so that the leakage of industrial secrets by employees is minimized.

Decisions for Handling Patent Disputes

As mentioned earlier, a principal component of China's patent protection system has been the reliance on administrative methods, rather than legal remedies, in patent infringement disputes. A patentee may request the administrative authority for patent affairs to handle the dispute or initiate legal proceedings directly in court. The administrative route has frequently been selected because it is widely available and faster, possibly resulting in raids on infringers within a matter of days. On another level, however, the use of this civil remedy for patent infringement goes against specifications of the TRIPS agreement (specifically Article 41[1]). Further, the AAPA is subject to conflicts of interest, since it issues the same patents that may be contended, and because of local or departmental protectionism, the impartiality of the AAPA in handling patent infringement disputes may be compromised.

The choice between administrative and legal routes to patent disputes will depend on several factors (Weldon & Vanhonacker, 1999). Administrative procedures are less expensive and less time consuming. They may be desired if an amicable relationship between the parties can be maintained, or if the dispute can be settled more thoroughly while at the same time protecting the interests of the patent holder. However, legal proceedings are usually more appropriate for patent disputes, since the cases may deal with larger amounts, are usually more complicated, and may lead to the invalidation of the patent in question. The yearly caseload of patent litigation cases is expected to more than double as a result of the 2001 amendments.

A further possibility of handling patent infringement exists through co-opting those who would violate patent protection rights. After unsuccessfully attempting to stop blatant replication of its motorcycle components in China, Honda Motor Corporation formed a joint venture in 2002 with one of the Chinese firms that had been imitating its products. The joint venture then began producing motorcycles for sale in China as well as for export to Japan. It was estimated that 70% of the motorcycles produced in China were unlicensed counterfeits bearing the designs and trademarks of Japanese products.

Other Patent Protection Decisions

The difference between first-to-invent and first-to-file is fundamental to the U.S. and Chinese patent systems. In the U.S., a company is entitled to an invention date as early as the date it can prove that it first conceived the invention – the date of conception. Under the Chinese system, patents are awarded to the company that first files a patent application. As a result, companies in China rarely developed the practice of documenting inventive activities because the Chinese Patent Office grants patents to the first to file an application embodying an invention rather than the party who proved they were the first to invent it. This is further affirmation that firms wishing to enter Chinese markets should register their patents in China prior to other investments. Registration through the Patent Cooperation Treaty also serves as a first-to-file mechanism, since an applicant in a PCT signatory nation receives priority in all PCT member countries. From the other side, however, firms undertaking innovation-related activities in China should document the development of inventions, to the point of keeping lab notes to determine the timing of inventorship and any disclosure (commercial use or publication) prior to application. U.S. law allows one year from date of disclosure for patent application.

With respect to patent category decisions, the Chinese three-category system seems to offer something for everyone. Invention patents are held to higher standards of inventiveness, since the claims are evaluated. Invention patents are also more expensive and time-consuming, but also offer broader and longer-term protection. The utility model was activated in order to provide access to the patent system for domestic, smaller applicants. The protection offered is narrower and enforcement is less stringent, but utility model patent costs are about half those of invention patents. A patent applicant might want to consider the degree of inventiveness involved in a product and file the appropriate application accordingly in order to increase the chances of being granted a patent. However, in order to increase the scope of protection, a business can simultaneously file an invention and a utility model patent application for the same product. Design patent protection is particularly important because infringement is equated with counterfeiting. While a design right does not protect technical product features, it does provide a product identity that links it to its manufacturer. Its protection can be similar to that involving a trademark, and designs would be particularly susceptible to passing off.

SUMMARY

The Chinese legal landscape continues to change rapidly. The fact that the country has set up an entirely new intellectual property system within the past twenty years is remarkable, and refinements to its system continue to be made. At the same time, however, the uncertainty of this system represents considerable risk to innovation-based firms. Unlike more developed countries, China's courts have not tested or applied much of the Patent Law, nor have they defined a great deal of the terminology used in the statute or its amendments beyond this first generation of patents. Therefore, extensive planning and the consideration of the local environment are compulsory for firms wishing to enter Chinese markets with inventive products.

Firms that sell highly technical, patentable products should be prepared to commit appropriate resources to protect their intellectual property in entering Chinese markets. In general, this would involve first seriously considering collaboration with an established intermediary, but then securing the appropriate protective contractual specifications in terms of the licensee's responsibilities in protecting the patent. Even though China has made significant progress in fostering an environment in which intellectual property rights are more likely to be protected, at this point it is recommended that firms with valuable intellectual property be proactive and preventative, rather than rely on legal recourses usually available in industrialized economies.

REFERENCES

Bloom, N., & Van Reenen, J. (2002). Patents, real options and firm performance. *Economic Journal*, *112*(478), C97–C116.

Burgel, O., & Murray, G. C. (2000). The international market entry choices of start-up companies in high-technology industries. *Journal of International Marketing*, *8*(2), 33–62.

China Intellectual Property Statistical Yearbook (2000). Beijing: Intellectual Property Publishing House.

China's new trademark policy is another sign of its intent to enter world trading systems (1979). *Business America*, *2*(10), 9.

Deng, Z., Lev, B., & Narin, F. (1999). Science and technology as predictors of stock performance. *Financial Analysts Journal*, *55*(3), 20–32.

Ernst, H. (1995). Patenting strategies in the German mechanical engineering industry and their relationship to company performance. *Technovation*, *15*(4), 225–242.

Ernst, H. (2001). Patent applications and subsequent changes of performance: Evidence from time-series cross-section analyses on the firm level. *Research Policy*, *30*(1), 143–157.

Hall, L. A., & Bagchi-Sen, S. (2002). A study of R&D, innovation, and business performance in the Canadian biotechnology industry. *Technovation*, *22*(4), 231–244.

How U.S. firm won patent suit in China (1997). *Crossborder Monitor*, August 6, 8.

Isobe, T., Makino, S., & Montgomery, D. B. (2000). Resource commitment, entry timing, and market performance of foreign direct investments in emerging economies: The case of Japanese international joint ventures in China. *Academy of Management Journal*, *43*(3), 468–484.

Kraar, L. (1985). China after Marx: Open for business? *Fortune*, *111*(4), 28–34.

Moga, T. T. (2001). China changes patent law to comply with TRIPS. *The National Law Journal*, *23*(48), C15.

Narin, F., Noma, E., & Perry, R. (1987). Patents as indicators of corporate technological strength. *Research Policy*, *16*(2–4), 143–156.

Sanyal, R. N., & Guvenli, T. (2001). American firms in China: Issues in managing operations. *Multinational Business Review* (Fall), 40–46.

Tse, D. K., Pan, Y., & Au, K. Y. (1997). How MNCs choose entry modes and form alliances: The China experience. *Journal of International Business Studies*, *28*(4), 779–805.

Weldon, E., & Vanhonacker, W. (1999). Operating a foreign-invested enterprise in China: Challenges for managers and management researchers. *Journal of World Business*, *34*(1), 94–107.

Yang, J. Z., Farley, J., & Hoenig, S. (1999). When MNCs come to China, who changes whom? *China Business Review*, *26*(2), 16–19.

Yu, J. (1991). Review of patent infringement litigation in the People's Republic of China. *Journal of Chinese Law*, *5*, 297–347.

Yu, P. K. (2000). From pirates to partners: Protecting intellectual property in China in the twenty-first century. *American University Law Review*, *50*(October), 131–243.

Zacharakis, A. L. (1997). Entrepreneurial entry into foreign markets: A transactions cost perspective. *Entrepreneurship Theory & Practice*, *21*(Spring), 23–29.

BUILDING STRATEGIC PARTNERSHIP BETWEEN MULTINATIONAL CORPORATIONS AND THEIR CHINESE COUNTERPARTS – A PRELIMINARY SURVEY WITH FOCUS ON EQUITY JOINT VENTURES

Chiang-nan Chao, Robert J. Mockler
and Dorothy G. Dologite

ABSTRACT

This research focuses on several important strategic concerns for multi-national corporations (MNCs) which are exploring strategic alliances in the China market. The results suggest that multinational corporations need to assess and re-assess continuously the business conditions in China, in order to understand this market better and be successful in future business dealings with China, a market that still has great growth potential. The significant differences exist between Western MNCs' executives and their Chinese counterparts. The results also suggest that MNCs should focus on joint venture partners' marketing capabilities, and bridge the differences between the joint venture partners.

Reviving Traditions in Research on International Market Entry
Advances in International Marketing, Volume 14, 125–139
Copyright © 2003 by Elsevier Science Ltd.
All rights of reproduction in any form reserved
ISSN: 1474-7979/doi:10.1016/S1474-7979(03)14007-0

INTRODUCTION

China's economy has maintained relatively healthy growth over the past three years, 7.1% in 1999, 8% in 2000, and 7.3% in 2001 (Bartels & Mirza, 1999; China National Bureau of Statistics, 2002; Sender, 2000; Wonacott, 2001). Based on real purchasing power, a method used by an *International Monetary Fund* review (Nomani, 1993), China's gross domestic product in 2001 reached about US$4.623 trillion, trailing only the U.S. and Japan. It is possible that by 2010 China could become the second largest economy in the world. The trade between China and the rest of the world in 2001 reached US$510 billion, an increase of 7.5% compared to 2000, down from a 24% increase in 1999. Many multinational corporations (MNCs) are facing ever growing global challenges at home and abroad, as economies in many countries are turning south, especially in the information technology sector. The worldwide foreign direct investments (FDI) have experienced sharp declines in many countries, for example, about 59% decline in the U.S. in 2001 (U.S. Bureau of Economic Analysis, 2002). However, China has experienced relatively stable FDIs during the same period, adding 14.9% in 2001, making China the second largest FDI recipient country only after the U.S. (China State Statistical Bureau, 2002; Dean, 2000; O'Neill, 2001). Such FDIs have generated about a half of China's total foreign trade since 1998 (MOFTEC FDI Statistics, 2002). Figure 1 compares FDIs in the U.S. and China for the past nine years.

REVIEW OF LITERATURE

Despite continuing economic reforms and generally improved foreign investment climate, doing business with China remains difficult (Calantone & Yushan, 2001; Garger, 2002; O'Neill, 2000; Peng & Luo, 2000; Roberts, 2000; Schlevogt, 2001; Tsang, 1998; Tung & Cho, 2000; Vanhonacker, 1997). MNCs have employed many different partnering strategies in China in the past years. Contractual agreements with Chinese corporations were favored when Chinese central planners controlled the economy. The contractual agreements involved little equity investment and offered MNCs a readily available market and distribution channels for specific products or rights. However, this form of strategic partnership lacks control to the MNCs.

Compensatory contracts, a form of strategic partnership in which foreign partners bring in equipment, materials, and/or management know-how in exchange for a predetermined quantity of finished products, were useful in the early 1980s for labor intensive manufacturing in China. In the mid-1980s, relatively

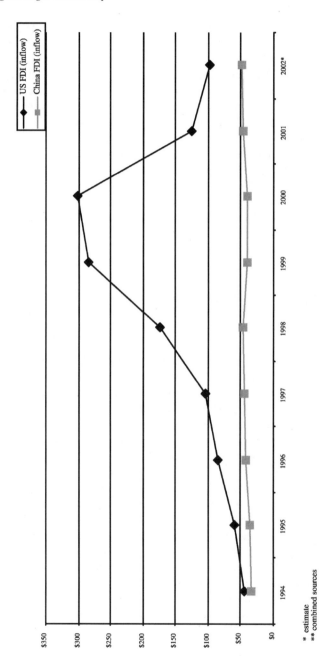

Fig. 1. FDIs in U.S. and China, US$ bil.*

* estimate
** combined sources

small-scale joint ventures of a few million U.S. dollar investment proved to be practical and less risky. For example, DaimlerChrysler AG. (then American Motors Corp.) invested only US$8 million in a partnership with Beijing Jeep Corp., which assembled autos from the imported kits (Aiello, 1991). In the early 1990s, large-scale ventures requiring several hundred million U.S. dollar investment became popular. These included Volkswagen's partnership with Shanghai Auto Works and Changchun First Auto Works, Northern Telecom Ltd's partnership with the Ministry of Communication and Guangdong Provincial Government, and General Motor's Venture in Shanghai (China Custom Report, 2001; Keatley, 1993; Keller, 1994). Coca-cola, re-entered China in 1979, has to date invested over US$1.2 billion and established twenty-four bottling plants and twenty-seven production locations (Coca-Cola, 2002). Its local employment has grown to 14,000 (Coca-Cola, 2002). The breakup of the state monopoly in many industries and the Chinese government's permissions that foreign partners can gain controlling shares in a joint venture enable MNCs to have more forms of strategic alliances to choose from, gain more control over the ventures, and turn ventures profitable (Forney, 2000b; Li, 2000; Reuters, 2000; Zhou, 2000). While many big MNCs, i.e. IBM, Intel, Nokia, and Motorola, are expanding their joint ventures in China in the recent years, wholly foreign-owned ventures and purchases of the stock of publicly traded Chinese corporations have also gained momentum (Forney, 2000a; Schlevogt, 2001).

Because of the restraints on data collecting, when conducting primary research in China, research on establishing strategic partnerships in China has been largely from the perspectives of the Western partners alone, or the Chinese counterparts alone (Calantone & Yushan, 2001; O'Neill, 2000; Roberts, 2000; Schlevogt, 2001). As a result, the research results have been substantially one-sided (Abramson & Ai, 1999; Nee, 1992; Shenkar, 1994). This study attempts to examine executives both in MNCs and their Chinese counterparts in their partnership. How do MNCs and their Chinese partners view the foreign direct investment conditions in China? What are the partners' reasons for establishing strategic partnerships? What are the strategic considerations for selecting desired strategic partners (Chan, 2000; Dologite, 1992; Flagg, 1999; Johnston & Lawrence, 1988; Landler, 1999; Leggett, 2000; Mockler, 1999). These are some of the key issues that many MNCs and their Chinese counterparts are concerned with in establishing a strategic alliance. This study hopes to provide MNCs with some insights for their globalization marketing strategies, and help gain a better understanding of both MNCs' and Chinese corporate executives' attitudes, practices, and preferences. This study also hopes to provide a base for future broader and more intensive studies.

RESEARCH DESIGN

Since the purpose of this research project was to better understand key issues for establishing strategic partnership between MNCs and their Chinese counterparts in the China market, the research questions were grouped to identify differing opinions between MNCs and their Chinese counterparts. This preliminary study intends to explore theories for further testing, refine testing instruments, and provide practical recommendations based on the test results.

Variable Selection and Measurement

The variables selected for this study reflect the key issues involved in building a strategic partnership with Chinese corporations (Calantone & Yushan, 2001; O'Neill, 2000; Peng & Luo, 2000; Roberts, 2000; Schlevogt, 2001; Tsang, 1998; Tung & Cho, 2000). These variables were structured in a questionnaire format. They were developed and grouped to examine the differing views between MNCs and their Chinese counterparts in this study. The questionnaire was then translated into Chinese using back translation tools to reduce errors. The English language and Chinese language versions of the questionnaires were initially distributed for testing and clarification to a small number of executives of MNCs and their Chinese counterparts, whom the researchers knew in their consulting practices and management training programs, in order to test and improve the usefulness and validity of the study. In-depth face-to-face interviews were also conducted to help refine the preliminary survey questions (Davis & Cosenza, 1985).

Dependent Variables
Three groups of dependent variables were selected to answer the research questions.

(1) *FDI conditions in China.* The executives participating in the study were asked to assess key aspects of foreign direct investment conditions using the five point Likert scale with five for best condition and one for worst condition. These variables covered business, economics, governmental, legal, financial, and political issues. These variables are summarized in Table 2.

(2) *Reasons for establishing strategic partnership between MNCs and their Chinese counterparts.* The participating executives were asked to indicate the reasons, in terms of their relative importance, for strategic partnering in

China market. A five-point Likert scale with five for most important and one for least important was used. These variables are summarized in Table 3.

(3) *Strategic partner selection considerations from both Western executives and their Chinese counterparts.* The participating executives were asked to evaluate the partner selection criteria in terms of their relative importance on a five point Likert scale with five for strongest and one for weakest. These variables are summarized in Table 4.

(4) *Independent Variables.* Two groups of executives from MNCs and their Chinese counterparts were the independent variables in this study.

Hypotheses

Three hypotheses were generated for testing the similarities and differences of the views between Western MNC executives and their Chinese counterparts, based on the literature review.

H1. There is no significant difference between Western MNC executives and their Chinese counterparts over foreign direct investment conditions in China.

H2. There is no significant difference between the Western MNC executives and their Chinese counterparts of the reason for establishing strategic alliances in China.

H3. There is no significant difference between the Western MNC executives and their Chinese counterparts regarding the partner selection strategies.

Test of Hypotheses

Since the independent variables were of a nominal nature and dependent variables were of ordinal nature, Mann–Whitney (Appendix) non-parametric statistic tests were used to test the hypotheses. The Mann–Whitney U (M–W U) test, often referred to as the rank sum test, was applied to test the null hypotheses. If the null hypotheses that the two samples were drawn from the same population were true, the totals of the ranks (or equivalently, the mean ranks) of the two samples would be expected to be about the same (Conover, 1980; Davis & Cosenza, 1985; SPSS[X], 2002). Five percent of *the* Mann–Whitney two-tailed probability level was selected to signify the differences between the two groups of executives.

Sample Used in the Preliminary Study

The target sample was a selected group of corporate or division level CEOs work-ing in foreign direct investment and operations for Western MNCs and Chinese corporations in China. The sample was screened from the Directories of American Business in China, 1999 (American Business in China, 1998–1999). Once the CEOs at corporate or division levels were identified, their Chinese partners were identified.

The English version questionnaires were distributed to the MNC executives whose headquarters were in a Western country. The Chinese version questionnaires were distributed to the executives in companies and agencies operating principally in China, regardless of what language they spoke. In this way, the two groups were distinct as related to at least one key variable in the study.

RESULTS

A total of nine hundred and eighty two survey questionnaires were sent to rela-tively equal numbers of Western MNC executives and their Chinese counterparts. One hundred sixty one executives returned surveys that were completed and used for this research. This represented about a 16% response rate. Of these respondents, fifty-nine were Western executives, while the remaining were Chinese executives. The background information about these executives and their industries is presented in Table 1.

Table 2 presents the M–W U results of foreign direct investment conditions in China market and two-tailed probabilities of M–W U tests from both MNC and Chinese respondents. The two groups significantly differ over *Government officials' bureaucracy, and red tape, Local content requirements, Chinese internal controls (unpublished)*, and *import/export controls (published)*. Therefore, the first null hypothesis is rejected. The test results indicate that the respondents significantly differ in their assessments of the foreign direct investment condition variables selected. Despite the fact that China has opened its doors to foreign investment for over twenty years, and has become a member country in the World Trade Organization, there is still a considerable amount of government controls over the economy, even though government officials there promote the idea of a free market economy in China widely. This is confirmed by several published analyses of the subject (Chen & Barshes, 2000; Einhorn et al., 2002; Garger, 2002; Steinfeld, 2000).

Table 3 presents the M–W U Z test results identified by both MNC respondents and their Chinese counterparts of the reason why they should establish a strategic

Table 1. The Executives' Background.

Items	Western	Chinese
Titles, executives	44%	21%
Titles, managers or directors	56%	61%
Titles, others	0%	19%
Titles, total	100%	100%
Industry types, Manufacturers	22%	32%
Industry types, Service	61%	40%
Industry types, others	17%	28%
Industry types, total	100%	100%
Education (4 = graduate degrees, 3 = college degrees)[a]	4	3
Foreign work experience (years)[a]	12	8
All work experience[a]	17	23
Total number of employees[a]	37,911	6,812
Expatriates in partner's country[a]	79	92
Total assets, in million of US$[a]	$81,311	$464
Investment in partner country, in millions of US$[a]	$121	$20
Sales last year, in millions of US$[a]	$48,101	446
Sales in partner country, last year, in millions of US$	154	78

[a] The average of all the respondents in the perspective group.

partnership. The two-tailed probabilities of M–W U tests indicate that there are significantly different views on the reasons why MNCs and their Chinese counterparts should establish strategic alliances. Therefore, the second null hypothesis is rejected. The rejection further suggests that there are significant

Table 2. Executives' View of FDI Conditions in China.

Variables	M–W U	Z	Sig.
Chinese official bureaucracy	283	(3.25)	0.00
China's Local content requirements for FDI	265	(2.44)	0.01
Chinese internal controls (unpublished)	656	(2.77)	0.01
Import/export controls (published)	355	(2.16)	0.03
Inflation/deflation	899	(1.85)	0.06
Availability of investment funds	462	(1.53)	0.13
Chinese official corruption	933	(1.01)	0.31
Surcharges	502	(0.88)	0.38
Disputes between labor and management in joint ventures	973	(0.40)	0.69
Foreign currency availability	1147	(0.34)	0.73
High initial investment	562	(0.21)	0.84

Note: 2-tailed probabilities are based on the Mann–Whitney two-sample Z test statistics. The variables are ranked in ascending order of the significant levels.

Table 3. Reasons for Establishing Ventures in China Market.

Variables	M–W U	Z	Sig.
Attractive sales terms	135	(3.47)	0.00
China does not produce, nor has substitute	459	(2.42)	0.02
China market size and potential	1009	(2.40)	0.02
Investment promotion	306	(1.96)	0.05
Economic growth	1106	(1.78)	0.07
Enable to expand your business	348	(1.58)	0.11
Fall into the scope of Chinese government's plans	396	(1.08)	0.28
Western made have high quality	538	(1.08)	0.28
Attractive sales prices	487	(1.07)	0.28
Can be profitable	532	(0.76)	0.45
Complete product lines	474	(0.61)	0.54
Advanced designs	545	(0.31)	0.76
On time delivery	508	(0.30)	0.76
Attractive packaging	503	(0.25)	0.80

Note: 2-tailed probabilities are based on the Mann–Whitney two-sample Z test statistics. The variables in bold indicate the significant levels of 5%. The variables are ranked in ascending order of the significant levels.

differences between the two groups of respondents in relation to their answers to *Attractive sales terms, China does not produce, nor has substitute, China market size and potential*, and *Investment promotion*. The rejection of the second null hypothesis indicates that Western respondents view these variables as less important when compared with their Chinese counterparts. Emphasis on *Product is not available in China market* can be an important strategy for MNCs when negotiating with potential Chinese partners and in getting the venture approved by government authorities relatively quickly.

The two-tailed probabilities of M–W U tests indicate that there are significantly different views on strategic partner selection variables between the MNC executives and their Chinese counterparts. Therefore, the third null hypothesis is rejected. The rejection of this hypothesis indicates that Western MNC executives differ significantly from their Chinese executives. The two groups differ particularly in *Have profit sense, Can market in China, Strong finance capability, High market share, and Strong connections in China*. The Western executives give a much higher rankings than the Chinese executives to the first two variables *Have profit sense* and *Can market in China*, while the Chinese executives view the last three variables as more important than the Western executives. It appears that the Western executives focus their strategic partner selection on the Chinese partners' capability to market the venture products in China, and the venture partners

Table 4.   Select Partners: Western and Chinese Executives' View.

Variables	M–W U	Z	Sig.
Have profit sense	649	(3.04)	0.00
Can market in China	729	(2.55)	0.01
Strong finance capability	399	(2.29)	0.02
High market share domestically and globally	319	(2.27)	0.02
Strong connections in China	796	(2.15)	0.03
Can hire and fire employees	824	(1.86)	0.06
Can choose locations freely	425	(1.72)	0.08
Hire Chinese as representatives	441	(1.63)	0.10
Understand ways of doing business in China	906	(1.62)	0.11
Have advance technology	446	(1.54)	0.12
Can export venture's products	458	(1.44)	0.15
Have customer service net works	358	(1.33)	0.19
Have advanced products	465	(1.03)	0.30
Have skilled workers	561	(0.87)	0.38
Competent managers	1066	(0.73)	0.47
Can obtain loans	1086	(0.61)	0.54
Wish and can transfer technology	630	(0.36)	0.72
Have reputation in China	1143	(0.28)	0.78
Internationally reputable	662	(0.14)	0.89
Speak Chinese and understand China	631	(0.14)	0.89
Have brand name product	522	(0.13)	0.90

Note: 2-tailed probabilities are based on the M–W two-sample Z test statistics. The variables in bold indicate the significant levels of 5%. The variables are ranked in ascending order of the significant levels.

should have a strong sense of making profit, the key point to the success of the foreign direct investment. On the other hand, the Chinese executives view the strong financial and market positions as more important, given their own strong connections within the China market. These results are shown in Table 4.

DISCUSSIONS

Since this study is of a preliminary nature, it has many limitations. For example, in addition to the issues covered in this preliminary survey, there are many other issues, which MNCs are concerned with. China is still not a free market economy, since many deals have to be approved by many layers of the Chinese central and local planners. An entry ticket to the World Trade Organization may not ensure MNC corporations fair competition with domestic Chinese companies. Continuing changes in business environment, economic reforms, and the directions of government policy makers force MNCs to constantly modify their strategies in China market as time passes.

Despite its limitations, the study compares the different views from both MNC executives and their Chinese counterparts, and can provide more comprehensive understandings for establishing a strategic partnership in China market. The study addresses several key issues in doing business with China today and provides some insights for strategic marketing formulation in the China market. The focuses should be placed on these differences between the Western executives and their Chinese counterparts.

The variables studied from both Western and Chinese respondents' points of view, indicate that the higher the rankings, the more critical and important of the variables in terms of building strategic partnerships between MNCs and their Chinese counterparts. This survey transmits a strong message to the MNCs that the primary reasons for building partnerships with their Chinese counterparts rests on many factors: *Attractive sales terms, China does not produce nor has substitute, China market size and potential, Investment promotion, and Economic growth.*

The rejections of the null hypotheses suggest that significant differences exist between Western MNC executives and their Chinese counterparts. For the successful launch of a foreign direct investment, the first step then is to objectively and fairly assess the foreign investment environment in China. Both Western MNC and Chinese executives rank *China market size and potential and Economic growth* the highest reason for investment. The Western MNC executives rank *Attractive sales terms* and *Investment promotion* higher than their Chinese counterparts. The Chinese executives rank *China does not produce nor has substitute, and China market size and potential* higher than their Western partners. First, Western respondents rank *Attractive sales terms* and *Investment promotion* significantly higher than their Chinese counterparts; as one respondent put it: venture's products would gain recognition quicker than the local brands, and a venture partner would be able to raise the prices comparably higher or much higher than the domestically-made Chinese products. One Western respondent replied that a venture partner could necessarily promote his company's presence, sales, and image in China. This Westerner believed that a partnership was a useful market access strategy, as fewer restrictions were imposed on the venture's products that were classified as domestically-made products, as compared to imports that are subject to heavy import duties and tariffs. This suggests that MNCs may need to reassess their market access strategies and give less emphasis to a self-serving reason such as giving the Westerners access to China market when negotiating to form a partnership with a Chinese corporation.

Second, Chinese respondents believe that *China does not produce nor has substitute, and China market size and potential* are more important considerations in forming partnerships than their Western counterparts, since they give these variables higher rankings. An emphasis on these variables can send favorable messages to the authorities from which approval is sought. This finding suggests that MNCs can gain strategic preference by emphasizing these issues when negotiating venture partnerships with their Chinese counterparts.

The high rankings of the Chinese partners' strengths by both the Western and Chinese respondents include: *Have reputation in China, Can obtain loans, Competent managers*, and *Understand ways of doing business in China*. The high rankings suggest that these are strategic factors for MNCs to emphasize. Finding a Chinese partner with strong profit sense and who can market venture products in China are of greater importance to the Western executives in contrast to the Chinese executives. The survey results confirm other findings by the authors, which suggest that Chinese managers still do not realize that their managerial skills lag behind what is expected from their Western counterparts (Delener & Chao, 1998).

Based on this preliminary survey, MNCs might consider focusing on those important issues derived in this preliminary study to formulate their approach to strategic partnering with Chinese corporations, even though further testing of the conclusions seems warranted. The following issues deserve special attention and careful evaluation for MNCs:

- Straight export products to China these days without forming a partnership with a Chinese corporation remains problematic, given China's market size, potential, and less than free market environment. Partnering with Chinese corporations is a necessary initial step to crack this vast market. In addition, such partnerships can, to a certain extent, protect MNC interests in China.
- When a Western company is planning to establish a partnership with a Chinese corporation: once such a plan becomes a reality and the Western partner's investment is in place, it is extremely difficult for the Western partner to withdraw his investment from the venture, even if the partnership turns sour. Liquidation alternatives are not readily available since the capital market in China is still in the developing phase. Perhaps in the future more Western partners will be able to sell their holdings to other buyers. So partner selection is the first and foremost critical issue in doing business in China. Finding a reliable and reputable partner can help ease potential problems.
- One approach for MNCs is to invest technology, management know-how, and equipment in a venture partnership, and then source locally and market locally and abroad.
- Merging with and acquiring public traded Chinese enterprises, by purchasing the equity shares in the open market, can be a realistic way to acquire a

partnership. This approach is gaining popularity in the past years, as the Chinese security exchange regulatory body has lifted some restrictions on foreign ownership (Bradsher, 2002).

A final observation during our many years in studying strategic partnering between MNCs and their Chinese counterparts is that in China nothing is impossible; as China is a big market, both law-making bodies at the central and local levels sometimes make conflicting rules and regulations. As for the implementation of venture strategies, it may work in one province, and not work in another.

REFERENCES

Abramson, N. R., & Ai, J. X. (1999). Canadian companies doing business in China: Key success factors. *Management International Review, 39*(1), Internet Edition.

Aiello, P. (1991). Building a joint venture in China: The case of Chrysler and the Beijing Jeep Corporation. *Journal of General Management, 17*(2), 47–63.

American Business in China (1999). 1998–1999, 2nd ed., Caravel, Inc.

Bartels, F., & Mirza, H. (1999). Multinational corporations foreign direct investment in Asia's emerging markets: Before and after the crisis-any changes? *Management International Review, 39*(4).

Bradsher, K. (2002). China expected to sell stakes to foreign companies. *NY Times*, Internet Edition, August 30.

Calantone, R. J., & Yushan, S. Z. (2001). Joint ventures in China. *Journal of International Marketing, 9*(1), 1.

Chan, C. (2000). CCT unwinds banned deals. *The South China Morning Post*, Internet Edition, February 2.

Chen, X., & Barshes, W. (2000). To team or not to team? *China Business Review*, Internet Edition, March–April.

China Custom Report (2001). Ministry of Foreign Trade and Economic Corporations Website.

China National Bureau of Statistics (2002).

Coca-Cola (2002). Company's source. http://english.peopledaily.com.cn/200107/27/eng20010727_75935.html http://www.chinabusinessreview.com/0107/weisert.html

Conover, W. J. (1980). *Practical nonparametric statistics*. New York: John Wiley & Sons.

Davis, D., & Cosenza, R. M. (1985). *Business research for decision making*. Boston: Kent.

Dean, J. (2000). Foreign direct investment in China fell 12% in 1999. *Dow Jones Newswires*, Internet Edition, January 13.

Delener, N., & Chao, C. N. (1998). Global challenges to joint ventures in China – the insight views of U.S. and Chinese CEOs. *Journal of Emerging Markets, 3*(2), 61–80.

Dologite, D. G. (1992). Expert systems to support strategic management decision making. *International Review of Strategic Management*. London: Wiley.

Einhorn, B., Himelstein, B. L., & Port, O. (2002). High tech in China. *Business Week*, Internet Edition, October 28.

Flagg, M. (1999). In fast-shifting China, Pepsi gains on Coca-Cola by picking its battles. *The Wall Street Journal*, Internet Edition, November 26.

Forney, M. (2000a). Motorola wins accord to make chips in China. *The Wall Street Journal*, Internet Edition, August 22.

Forney, M. (2000b). China's loosening telecom sector has room for careful newcomers government involvement limits even independent data services. *The Wall Street Journal*, Internet Edition, August 29.

Garger, I. (2002). Interview with Ezra Vogel on China-Japan relations. *Harvard Asia Quarterly*, August.

Johnston, R., & Lawrence, P. R. (1988). Beyond vertical integration – the rise of the value-adding partnership. *Harvard Business Review* (July–August), 94–101.

Keatley, R. (1993). U.S. firms, anticipating huge market, worry China may lose its MFN status. *The Wall Street Journal*, May 14, A10.

Keller, J. J. (1994). Northern Telecom signs accord to set up operations in China. *The Wall Street Journal*, April 25, B6.

Landler, M. (1999). Buicks are making inroads in China. *New York Times*, Internet Edition, December 9.

Leggett, K. (2000). China opens energy grid to limited competition. *The Wall Street Journal*, Internet Edition, January 28.

Li, R. (2000). Foreign firms report combined 6b yuan profits. *South China Morning Post*, Internet Edition, September 13.

Mockler, R. J. (1999). *Multinational strategic alliances*. New York: John Wiley & Sons.

MOFTEC FDI Statistics (2002). http://www.chinafdi.gov.cn/english/O1/f/26/27.htm

Nee, V. (1992). Organizational dynamics of market transition: Hybrid firms, property rights, and mixed economy in China. *Administrative Science Quarterly, 31*, 1–27.

O'Neill, M. (2000). Stronger economy delivers windfall. *South China Morning Post*, Internet Edition, January 12.

O'Neill, M. (2001). Data paints distorted picture as state sector struggles. *South China Morning Post*, Internet Edition, January 20.

Peng, M. W., & Luo, Y. (2000, June). Managerial ties and firm performance in a transition economy: The nature of a micro-macro link. *Academy of Management Journal, 43*(3), 486–501.

Reuters (2000). Beijing to allow foreign control in joint ventures. *Reuters*, Shanghai, Internet Edition, September 11.

Roberts, D. (2000). Tuning up a Chinese clunker (international edition). *Business Week*, Internet Edition, January 17.

Schlevogt, K. A. (2001). *The art of Chinese management*. Oxford University Press.

Sender, H. (2000). Some are starting to bet on broad China recovery. *The Wall Street Journal*, Internet Edition, January 18.

Shenkar, O. (1994). The people's Republic of China raising the bamboo screen through international management research. *International Studies of Management and Organizations, 24*(1/2), 9–34.

Steinfeld, E. S. (2000). Free lunch or last supper? China's debt-equity swaps in context. *China Business Review*, Internet Edition, July–August.

SPSS^X 2002. http://www.spss.com

Tsang, E. W. K. (1998). Can Guanxi be a source of sustained competitive advantage for doing business in China? *Academy of Management Executive, 12*(2), 64–73.

Tung, S., & Cho, S. (2000). The impact of tax incentives on foreign direct investment in China. *Journal of International Accounting Auditing & Taxation, 9*(2), 105.

U.S. Bureau of Economic Analysis (2002). http://www.bea.doc.gov/bea/di/di1fdibal.htm

Vanhonacker, W. (1997). Entering China: An unconventional approach. *Harvard Business Review, 75*(2), 130–140.

Wonacott, P. (2001). Forced holidays may not help revive China's ailing economy. *The Wall Street Journal*, Internet Edition, January 26.

Zhou, J. (2000). Ericsson teams up with China unicom. *South China Morning Post*, Internet Edition, August 24.

APPENDIX

The Mann–Whitney procedure is used to test whether two independent samples have been drawn from populations having the same mean. Hence, the rank sum test may be viewed as a substitute for the parametric t-test or the corresponding large-sample normal curve test for the difference between two means. If any difference between the two population distributions is due only to the difference in location of the two distributions, then the Mann–Whitney test is equivalent to testing whether or not the two population means are equal. This is similar to the two independent sample t-test, where we must assume that the two population variances are equal.

The Mann–Whitney test is based on the notion that if the two independent random samples have been drawn from the same population, then the average of the sample ranks $r(x_i)$ and $r(y_i)$ should be approximately equal. If the average of the $r(x_i)$ is much greater or smaller than the average of the $r(y_i)$, then this indicates that the two samples likely came from different populations. In order to carry out the test, the Mann–Whitney statistic U is calculated. This test statistic depends only on the number of items in the samples and the total of the ranks in one of the samples. It is defined as follows:

$$U = n_1 n_2 + \frac{n_1(n_1 + 1)}{2} R_1$$

The statistic U provides a measurement of the difference between the ranked observations of the two samples and yields evidence about the difference between the two population distributions. Very large or very small U values constitute evidence of the separation of the ordered observations of the two samples. Under the null hypothesis stated earlier, it can be shown that the sampling distribution of U has a mean equal to

$$u_U = \frac{n_1 n_2}{2}$$

and a standard deviation of

$$U = \frac{n_1 n_2 (n_1 + n_2 + 1)}{12}$$

Furthermore, it can be shown that the sampling distribution approaches normality very rapidly and may be considered approximately normal when both n_1 and n_2 are in excess of about ten (Hamburg, 1977, p. 530).

ENABLERS OF LONG-TERM MARKETING RELATIONSHIPS IN CROSS-CULTURAL BUSINESS

Angelica C. Cortes and Arturo Vasquez-Parraga

ABSTRACT

This paper aims at advancing research on the identification and the first test of the primary steps companies follow to generate and maintain enablers of long-term marketing relationships in cross-cultural business. To achieve the objective, the authors first identify the communication difficulties in generating and maintaining long-term relationships in bi-cultural or multi-cultural settings. They then develop the building blocks, or enablers, that are needed to form and maintain enduring relationships. They finally illustrate the suggested process by describing the use of enablers in two contrasting cultures, the Anglo-Saxon and the Latin, using samples from the United States and Chile, respectively.

INTRODUCTION

The core of relationship marketing for companies is the realization that long-lasting relationships are more valuable than a series of short-term relationships in which customers, suppliers, or distributors must be continually replaced. Because they avoid the inefficiencies inherent in constant searches, stable relationships maintained over the long-term, increase effectiveness and promote

Reviving Traditions in Research on International Market Entry
Advances in International Marketing, Volume 14, 141–168
ISSN: 1474-7979/doi:10.1016/S1474-7979(03)14008-2

efficiency (Reichheld, 1996). It is this recognition that has made relationship marketing an important requirement for a high level of company performance (Barlow, 1992).

The bulk of research in relationship marketing has focused on defining relationship marketing and in identifying the types of business where it is useful: consumer, business-to-business, manufacturing, financing, etc. More specifically, research has focused on the contribution of relationship marketing to the performance of business firms, the changes in the organizational culture that requires the adoption and implementation of relationship marketing, and the necessary technology (Berry, 1983).

A vast literature on relationship marketing exists, as evidenced by the work presented in the *Annual Relationship Marketing Colloquium* (10th edition) and the *Annual IMP Conference* (17th edition), but important information is still missing from this extensive corpus. Still needed, for instance, is the identification of the elements that help develop long-lasting relationships, and, more importantly, ascertaining the primary steps or building blocks that make possible both the formation and the maintenance of long-term relationships between business firms.

This paper aims at advancing research on the identification and description of the primary steps that enable the formation and maintenance of relationship marketing. First, we focus on: (a) the communication processes, with emphasis on the set of social codes that govern business interactions and which facilitate or preclude the generation and maintenance of long-term business relationships; and (b) the role of trust and commitment, two factors found to be prerequisites for establishing long-term relationships (Hunt & Morgan, 1994; Parasuraman et al., 1991). Second, we develop the building blocks, or enablers, that are needed to generate and maintain enduring relationships.

The scope of this research is limited to business-to-business relationships in the financial industry. The cross-cultural business application is limited to two points of reference as exemplified by the comparison of an Anglo-Saxon culture (the United States) with a Latin culture (Chile). It has been widely recognized by researchers such as Hofstede (1980), Hickson and Pugh (1995), and Triandis et al. (1988), among others, that the Anglo-Saxon culture is the dominant culture of the United States, and the Latin culture is the dominant culture of Chile. The research presented here is based on the dominant cultures of the respective countries.

First, we summarize current knowledge about relationship marketing in the context of cross-cultural business-to-business relationships. Then, on the basis of the existing literature and qualitative research, we describe the enablers of relationship marketing. Finally, we illustrate the use of the enablers by performing quantitative research on financial companies in the two selected, contrasting cultures.

ESTABLISHING MARKETING RELATIONSHIPS IN CROSS-CULTURAL BUSINESS

Although the literature on relationship marketing is abundant, most of it is normative (Hincks, 2002). Only a handful of studies address the conceptual foundations of relationship marketing (Sheth & Parvatiyar, 2000). And only a few of this small group defines relationship marketing and discusses the benefits of engaging in it. When these benefits are discussed, they are viewed from either a narrow or a broad perspective. From a narrow perspective, relationship marketing is limited to databases for use in marketing's promotional efforts, as tools for enhancing customer retention efforts, and as an aid in developing strategies for maintaining customer bonding. From a broad perspective, relationship marketing is used to develop and maintain networks of customers, with the expectation that such networks will be beneficial to both the consumers and the company.

And then there is relationship marketing as a strategic component. In this context it is viewed as a tool utilized in the pursuit of goals and objectives. Some authors see it as Total Quality Management (TQM), where customer satisfaction is a salient priority and where, therefore, initiating and maintaining genuine communication with customers is an important role of marketing (Gummesson, 1987; Sheth & Parvatiyar, 2000; Triandis, Botempo et al., 1988). Other authors value the role of relationship marketing for what they see as its capability for maintaining and enhancing long-term customer relationships (Rosenber & Czepiel, 1984). Most applications of relationship marketing are found in business-to-business relationships, particularly channels (Varadarajan & Cunningham, 1995). Nevertheless, some applications are also found in consumer relationships (Sheth & Parvatiyar, 2000). Our research addresses business-to-business relationships that take place in cross-cultural contexts.

Business-to-business relationships in cross-cultural contexts become increasingly more difficult, partly because communication is becoming more complex in today's world, and partly because the international business community lacks effective tools to address communication problems. Both factors can easily undermine the efforts of business representatives to generate and/or maintain relationships. We first address the communication challenges, and then discuss the tools needed to develop effective communication in cross-cultural business-to-business relationships.

Communication Challenges in Cross-Cultural
Business-to-Business Relationships

The first challenge experienced by business organizations in the development of relationship marketing across cultures is establishing effective communication. Business organizations do not exist in isolation from the cultures in which they originate or exist; they are created and run by people who bring with them the values, norms, attitudes, and beliefs that reflect the surrounding national culture (Tayeb, 1992).

Moreover, the type of industry in which an organization operates and the corporate culture that the firm cultivates often become mediating factors in the establishment of successful cross-cultural communications. O'Hara-Devereaux and Johansen (1994), following Hall's (1959) perspective, assert that communication differs in the context of industries or company functions. Companies focused on marketing and sales to firms in a different culture, for example, are expected to understand, accept, and accommodate their customers' views, however alien they might seem. Firms such as these are characterized as high-context organizations, and the failure to understand the demands created by operating in a high-context environment can lead to disastrous communication difficulties. Conversely, companies focused on finance are expected to value analytical thinking and precision. These firms are categorized as low-context organizations, and again, a failure to fully comprehend the requirements of doing business in a low-context organization can also lead to significant communication failures.

O'Hara-Devereaux and Johansen (1994) argue that a low-context industry is conservative, formal, analysis-oriented, emphasizes explicit communication and the use of precise data. A financial organization, by the nature of its business, seems to have a strong dependence on written contracts, a high degree of confidentiality in the use of client information, and strict ethical norms in business conduct. In contrast, a high-context organization emphasizes functional areas such as marketing, sales, human resources, and manufacturing. These firms are characterized by larger networks and the need to forge bonds with their clients that develop into personal friendships that generate trust and personal commitments to the business relationship. By the nature of their business, high-context organizations seem to be less reliant on written contracts. They give greater importance to understanding the customers' views, and recognize a greater need for collaboration on joint projects. The more distance between the two types of organizations in the low to high-context continuum, the more dissimilar their approach to business relationships, the greater the potential for significant communication failures.

The potential for communication difficulties in business resulting from this high-low context distinction is a reflection of what happens in national cultures generally. The more diverse two cultures are on this continuum, the more complex will be their communication (Hall, 1959, 1976). Moreover, there is substantial evidence of the difficulties inherent in the communication between points distant along this continuum, specially when people belong to different cultures, as reported by Hall and Hall (1990), and Graham (1985, 1987). Despite the recognition that communication is very important and difficult across cultures, little effort has been made to identify the mechanisms that can establish and maintain effective communication channels between people of different cultures. Thus, we pose our first research question:

RQ1. In a given industry, what are the mechanisms business people of one culture use to establish successful communication and develop relationships with business people of another culture?

The second challenge is the process of communication, particularly the identification of the strategies needed to make it successful in the long-term. One of the central concerns is the development and maintenance of trust beyond the superficial relationships of formal business practices. A number of communication strategies used by the channel members, for instance, have been identified and described by researchers in channel relationships. Some of these strategies are based on aggressive negotiation between the partner and/or the use of positions of power to gain advantages in the relationship (Frazier et al., 1989). But there clearly is a growing interest in efforts to adopt non-coercive tactics, more collaborative approaches, and a long-term orientation in the practice of negotiations in order to create a supportive working environment (Frazier et al., 1989; Ganesan, 1993; Weitz & Jap, 1995).

While some work has been done, there are still areas in the process that need to be studied, including: (a) the effectiveness of control mechanisms; (b) channel partners' attitudes and feelings toward the relationship; and (c) the communication models used in the relationship (Weitz & Jap, 1995). Weitz and Jap (1995) concluded that even when existing research provides insights into the communication used in channels of distribution, it does not provide answers as to how and why long-term relationships develop, nor does it address how these long-term relationships are maintained. Granted, the literature does underscore the importance of developing long-term relationships (Gordon, 2000; Gummesson, 1987; Morgan, 2000; Sisoda & Wolfe, 2000), but it stops short of pointing out how long-term relationships are generated; identifying the building blocks of long-term relationships; and, more specifically, explaining how relationships that are first recognized are cultivated, nurtured and/or periodically refreshed so as to become long-term business relationships.

Thus, we need to examine closely the process by which long-term relationships are generated, maintained, and/or enhanced. More specifically, we need to identify the enablers, or instrumental agents, that make the relationships possible, viable, and valuable. Enablers work as prerequisites, or builders, of long-term relationships, but they can vary according to the characteristics of the social actors involved in building and reaffirming the relationship. Thus, we are led to our next research question:

RQ2. What are the enablers that business people use to maintain long-term relationships with business people from different cultures? What is the nature and scope of those enablers?

Both questions can be answered by identifying and elaborating on the enablers of long-term relationships in cross-cultural businesses.

Enablers of Long-Term Relationships in Cross-Cultural Business

Most researchers agree that cultural factors, more than any other type of factors, are most critical in cross-cultural long-term relationships (Brislin, 1981; Hickson & Pugh, 1995; Hofstede, 1980; Tayeb, 1996; Triandis, Botempo et al., 1988). Cultural factors identify the different ways people from different cultures approach communication, negotiation, agreement or disagreement, etc., as a result of engaging in a relationship for purposes of mutual interest. A significant component of such factors is made up of business protocols, the cultural scripts people use to approach others, particularly when the counterpart of the communication belongs to a different culture. Consider for a moment the communication difficulties that could arise when one person who comes from a self-oriented culture tries to communicate with another who comes from a group-oriented society.

Some business protocols are used to build relationships, whereas others are used to maintain relationships. The business protocols that relate to the formation stage of long-term relationships in cross-cultural business include: (a) the manners in which the social actors establish the relationship; (b) the significance of time-related values such as punctuality and the importance of deadlines; and (c) the perception and response to power and authority. The protocol of manners is connected to proxemics and the establishment of: (a) the appropriate social and table etiquettes; (b) the different ways people greet each other; and (c) the distance people observe in physical interaction and the adherence to certain criteria regarding appropriateness and adequacy of these distances. The protocol of time refers to the way people respect: (a) punctuality; and (b) adherence to deadlines. The protocol of power distance addresses differential power made visible by the way people relate to others and accept authority such as: (a) respecting organizational ranks; (b) addressing others by their first name or title; (c) dealing with disagreements; and (d) respecting organizational rules and managerial ranks.

The business protocols that support the maintenance stage of cross-cultural business relationships focus on bonding, which encompasses: (a) the maintenance of relationships; (b) the exchange of gifts; (c) client maintenance with a focus on friendship; and (d) loyalty. Bonding is related to the communication context and the boundaries a culture establishes as appropriate when developing friendships with clients.

What follows is an examination of the business norms and rules regarding those four groups of business protocols that influence either the formation or the maintenance of cross-cultural long-term business-to-business relationships. We first present the protocols that relate to the formation of relationships – manners, time, and power distance – then follow up with a discussion of the protocol of bonding, which is concerned with the maintenance of relationships.

BUSINESS PROTOCOLS ENABLING THE FORMATION OF LONG-TERM RELATIONSHIPS ACROSS CULTURES

Protocol of Manners

In the context of social interaction, "manners" refers to the way individuals carry themselves. These manners pertain to demeanor, table etiquette, and social grace (Burgoon et al., 1996). Manners and personal impressions are often connected. The practices associated with the protocol of manners are: (a) dress code and clothing style; (b) social and table manners; and (c) greetings.

"Dress code" refers to the standards set by the organization that define how employees should dress. It differs from clothing style, which refers to what is considered appropriate dress for each managerial level. Clothes do not make the executive, but they do affect how others perceive the individual independent of his or her position. Malandro et al. (1989) found that people have a high degree of accuracy when using clothing to judge others regarding sex, age, economic status, group membership, occupational status, and official status.

"Social and table manners" refers to the etiquette expected by the culture and the social group regarding how people conduct themselves in a social setting. Impression management (Burgoon et al., 1996) concerns manipulation of the verbal and non-verbal communication processes that one person engages in to create a positive image in the eyes of another.

Goffman (1959, 1976) uses the term "performance" to refer to the totality of non-verbal and verbal acts that are perceived to have social or cultural meanings and to help understand the mechanisms which influence the interpretations of another's behavior in a given situation. Performance comprises appearance (clothing and other symbols of an individual's social status), manners (interaction and attitudes toward the interaction as reflected in facial expressions, posture, and rate of movement), and setting (physical environment cues that place the interaction or situation in context).

"Greetings" refers to how people welcome and acknowledge one another in social and business settings, and how the regulatory functions they perform by signaling the beginning of the interaction (Knapp & Hall, 1997). Greetings also conveys information about the relationship between the people in the interaction such as providing signs of status differentials, intimacy, current feelings, and attitudes. Kendon and Ferber (1973) identify six stages in the performance of greetings: (a) sighting, orientation, and initiation of the approach; (b) the distant salutation, the "official ratification" of the greeting; (c) the head dip; (d) the approach; (e) the final approach; and (f) the closing salutation. In non-touching cultures, for instance, the closing salutation might be a bow, and in touching cultures, it might be a handshake or an embrace. Greetings also relates to Hall's study of proxemics (Hall, 1966), the physical distance that people maintain between themselves and another. This distance is culturally determined and culture bound, and it influences how people in a given culture feel about touching when greeting each other. An American, for instance, usually maintains a distance of between one and a half and four feet from another person in personal relationships, and a distance in social settings of between four and seven feet. In contrast, a Latin American is comfortable much closer to another.

Protocol of Time

"Time" refers to the value that a culture instills in its members regarding the management of time. Broadly put, differences in values are derived from a monochronic or polychronic sense of time (Hall, 1976, 1982). Monochronic time refers to a linear concept of time in which time is treated almost as a physical product. People with a monochronic sense of time tend to be schedule-driven, so much so that adhering to the schedule takes precedence over the completion of the task. Polychronic time is a more flexible notion of time. People with a polychronic sense of time tend to be more task-driven rather than schedule-driven, so they are somewhat more flexible regarding deadlines. Cultures with a monochronic conception of time perceive time as fixed and measurable, while polychronic cultures perceive time as fluid and multidimensional (Hall, 1976). Two practices are associated with the use of these time frames: (a) being punctual when appointments have been made; and (b) meeting deadlines and completing paperwork in a timely manner.

"Punctuality" refers to a sense of a respect for the time set for meetings. Attitudes toward time vary from culture to culture. The study of humans, their time systems, and how they structure and interpret time is known as chronemics (Malandro et al., 1989). Hall (1976) sees seven elements in conceptions of formal time: ordering, cyclicity, valuation, tangibility, synthesis, duration, and depth. From Hall's (1976) and Levine and Wolff's (1985) research, we learn that a culture's sense of valuation, tangibility, and duration of time is probably what exerts the greatest influence on an individual's ordering of time-related values and activities (punctuality and deadlines).

"Deadlines" refers to a sense of respect for times established for the completion of projects or reports. The issue of deadlines also relates to time perception at the cultural level. As with punctuality, ordering is relevant to deadlines because of the importance of time structuring to the sequence of certain events such as the scheduled time to work on reports and the completion of the paperwork necessary to meet established deadlines.

Protocol of Power Distance

"Power Distance" refers to how people within an organization feel about differential power and status associated with organizational ranks. The concept is derived from Hofstede's (1980) power distance, the inequality of status, power and the relationship between the manager and subordinates. Hofstede (1980) maintained that inequality within an organization's ranks is both necessary and functional. Business organizations do not operate without a line of authority that defines responsibility as well as accountability. Every culture prescribes different degrees of importance to power and status differentials. Key cultural prescriptions regarding power distance relate to: (a) the use of title or first-name calling; (b) company rules; (c) organizational rank; (d) scope of agreement and disagreement with supervisor; (e) superior's involvement; and (f) cordiality. Before proceeding, we should briefly define each of these terms.

The use of titles or first-name calling refers to the appropriateness of addressing another person by his or her first name during the first meeting. This behavior is one of the most common practices addressed by rules of business protocols and etiquette. Axtell (1985) and Copeland and Griggs (1985) observe that some Europeans and Latin Americans expect the use of their titles and degrees, and they do not use first names without an invitation. Moreover, some languages distinguish between a formal and informal "you" (e.g. Spanish and German), and they require a formal invitation to move from the use of a formal "you" to an informal "you." Such an invitation may never be offered in intercultural business interactions.

"Company rules" refers to formalization and centralization of power (Hall, 1991). Organizations with highly formalized procedures tend to insist on a rigid conformity to their rules, as opposed to the more flexible attitude toward rules that is found in more informal and decentralized organizations.

"Organizational rank" refers to the difference in status resulting from a difference in position within an organization. Burgoon et al. (1996) refer to the issue of inequality in business organizations that are governed by power, dominance, and status. "Power" refers to the ability to influence others, often resulting from the ability to control the distribution of resources. "Dominance" refers to behavioral patterns that influence others (Ridgeway et al., 1985). "Status" refers to the position within the organizational hierarchy. High status usually fosters power and dominance.

"Scope of agreement and disagreement with supervisor" refers to how comfortable subordinates feel in expressing disagreements with their supervisors. It also refers to the mechanisms provided by an organization that enable employees to express opinions and the system that the organization has – or lacks – for handling disagreements. The literature on the topic of the protocol of distance describes different attitudes among different cultural groups. Laurent (1983), for example, describes the notion common in business organizations in the United States that employees are colleagues rather than bosses and subordinates. Southern Europeans, on the other hand, operate in hierarchical structures where everyone in the organization knows who has authority over whom.

"Superior's involvement" refers to where on a democratic-autocratic continuum employees prefer their supervisors to place themselves. Hickson and Pugh (1995) and Tayeb (1992) assert that Anglo-Saxon managers tend to be more democratic and consultative, while Latin managers tend to be more autocratic, paternalist, and reliant on direct instructions. As a result, Anglo-Saxon subordinates are more likely to feel comfortable expressing disagreements with their managers, while Latin subordinates, who tend to work in autocratic environments, are more apt to feel uncomfortable about expressing disagreements with their superiors.

Finally, "cordiality" refers to social grace and the consideration one person shows for another in social and business settings. Cordiality, similar to Triandis's Simpatía Script, focuses on an individual's efforts to convey a positive image to others (Triandis et al., 1984). It is also linked to behaviors intended to inject an element of grace in business interactions by encouraging such behaviors as engaging in non-conflictive interactions, timing conversations so they are not initiated at inappropriate times, not pressing for business talks in social settings, and letting the host initiate a business discussion (Axtell, 1985; Copeland & Griggs, 1985).

BUSINESS PROTOCOLS ENABLING THE MAINTENANCE OF LONG-TERM RELATIONSHIPS ACROSS CULTURES

Protocol of Bonding

"Bonding" refers to the strength of the relationship established between the partners. Different cultures place different emphases on the need to establish and maintain a bond with a partner for the success of a business relationship. Bonding is studied in the context of communication (Hall, 1966), in-group/out-group research (Triandis, Botempo et al., 1988), and collectivism/individualism research (Hofstede, 1980).

High-context cultures, which seem to have large and numerous networks, emphasize the need to establish relationships before formalizing business arrangements (Hall, 1966), unlike low-context cultures, which have small and few networks, and whose approach to business is more legalistic. Collectivist cultures have many in-groups, so a business relationship, if it is to be successful, needs to begin with the cultivation of an in-group relationship and bonding before actually getting down to business (Hui & Triandis, 1986; Triandis, Brislin et al., 1988). Unlike collectivist cultures that tend to value the formation and maintenance of bonds among the people concerned, individualist cultures place more emphasis on the business contract (Hofstede, 1980). The establishment of bonds in the latter cultures is desirable but unnecessary. When and where it is desired, bonding is best achieved by cultivating appropriate practices in four areas: (a) gift-exchange; (b) maintenance of relationships; (c) client maintenance with focus on friendship; and (d) loyalty.

"Gift exchange" refers to the giving and receiving of gifts for business reasons. In different cultures, exchanging gifts can affirm or impair a business relationship. A gift may incur obligations, though repayment in kind may not be necessary. Dillon (1976) said that the major problem for U.S. business people regarding gifts is that they want to give gifts but do not want to receive them. Giving without receiving, Dillon notes, may place the other party in a disadvantageous position.

"Maintenance of relationships" is concerned with the frequency of contacts between partners in the process of establishing and maintaining a bond. The importance of bonding differs between a collectivist and individualist cultures (Hofstede, 1980). People in collectivist cultures belong to several in-groups that exert varying degrees of influence on an individual. The key to establishing a successful business relationship in a collectivist culture is obtaining entrance into one or more of a manager's in-groups first, then preserving membership by frequent contact (Triandis, Botempo et al., 1988). Conversely, people in individualist cultures belong to fewer in-groups and experience lesser difference between in-groups and out-groups. Because in-groups an individualist culture lack any special significance, at least as far as business relationships are concerned, they do not exert any much influence on individuals entrusted with making business decisions. Individualist cultures value personal independence and autonomy more than group membership, so establishing and maintaining relationships through frequent encounters and membership in a counterpart's in-group is less important than it is in a collectivist culture (Hall & Hall, 1990).

"Client maintenance with focus on friendship" refers to the closeness that provides depth to the relationship established between partners during the course of a long-term relationship. It implies a personal relationship within the boundaries of a given culture. Gudykunst and Lim (1986) argue that interpersonal and intergroup relationships smooth out business relationships by simplifying the communication process, facilitate people's awareness of the consequences of getting involved in interpersonal behaviors, and enable one partner to interpret and predict, with some degree of accuracy, the behavior and future actions of another. As a consequence, friendship that originates in client maintenance reduces the amount of uncertainty in the relationship. Berger and Calabrese (1975) point out that the primary concern when meeting someone for the first time is reducing uncertainty and the accompanying anxiety, especially if we will be meeting that person again. The more collectivist the society is, the more friendship is required as a way of avoiding uncertainty and anxiety. Conversely, in individualist societies, friendship may not be required to reduce the level of uncertainty in a new relationship.

"Loyalty" refers to the long-term commitment of partners in support of their personal and business relationship. It is subject to narrower boundaries in individualist cultures than it is in collectivist cultures. Loyalty in business develops well when the boundaries for friendship are wide and there is no perceived conflict of interest between a business relationship and a personal friendship. For example, business relationships in more collectivist cultures, such as the Latin culture, may require the personalization of the relationships and business contracts, the so-called "Latin touch," to counterbalance and soften the effects of hierarchical structures and bureaucratized systems (Hickson & Pugh, 1995). Conversely, business relationships in more individualist cultures, such as the Anglo-Saxon cultures, may rely more on written contracts to manage the business relationship than on personal contacts and friendship.

In summary, the four protocols extracted from the literature and described here are tools to either generate or maintain long-term business relationships. These protocols enhance communication between people that aim at exchanges over a prolonged period. Moreover, they facilitate relationships between cultures separated by different orientations such as high-context and low-context cultures, or collectivist and individualist cultures. What follows is an example of how these protocols work in relationships established across two distinct cultures, a Latin culture and an Anglo-Saxon culture.

BUSINESS PROTOCOLS AS ENABLERS OF RELATIONSHIP MARKETING IN TWO CONTRASTING CULTURES: ANGLO-SAXON vs. LATIN BUSINESS PEOPLE

Methodology

This research uses a combination of qualitative and quantitative methods in order to first identify the types of protocols used (qualitative) and, then to measure the extent to which those protocols were actually used in cross-cultural settings (quantitative). The qualitative study is guided by the research questions, whereas, the quantitative study is guided by the hypotheses.

The qualitative approach relies on in-depth interviews with twelve vice-presidents, six in the United States and six in the Chilean subsidiaries of those U.S. companies, involved in international business at financial companies. The interviews, which lasted about three hours each, were conducted over a period of six months by the researcher in the language of the interviewee (English or Spanish). Various themes and topics (see descriptors in Table 1) related to business protocols emerged from the content analysis of the interviews. These were carried over to the instruments developed for the quantitative phase of the research.

The financial companies chosen included four large U.S. banks and two large insurance companies that: (a) had similar operations and procedures in the United States and Chile; (b) were involved in business-to-business international business and consumer sales; and (c) provided access that enabled us to interview the executives in charge of business-to-business international business and survey the lower level managers involved in consumer sales. Both the qualitative and the quantitative studies showed that the banks and insurance companies were fundamentally similar. As part of the quantitative phase of the study, a semi-structured questionnaire that took into account the requirements necessary

Table 1. Correspondence Between Business Protocols and Resulting Factors.

Qualitative Analysis		Quantitative Analysis	
Protocols	Descriptors	Indicators	Factors
Manners	Dress Code		Manners
	Clothing Style	Clothing Style	
	Social Manners	Social Manners	
	Table Manners	Table Manners	
Time	Punctuality	Punctuality	Time
	Deadlines	Deadlines	
	Paperwork	Paperwork	
Power Distance	Titles or first name calling	Titles or first name calling	Power Distance
	Organizational Rank	Organizational Rank	
	Company's Rules	Company's Rules	
	Agreement with Supervisor	Supervisor Agreement	
	Disagreement with supervisor	Supervisor Disagreement	
	Superior's Involvement	Superior Involvement	
	Cordiality	Cordiality	
Bonding	Giving Gifts	Giving Gifts	Bonding
	Taking Gifts	Taking Gifts	
	Maintaining Relationships	Maintaining Relationships	
	Client Maintenance	Client Maintenance	
	Loyalty		

for achieving three basic levels of equivalence, namely construct equivalence, measurement equivalence, and equivalence of data collection techniques (Singh, 1995) was developed and distributed to the bank branch managers and insurance agents of the organizations whose executives were interviewed in the qualitative phase. The questionnaire, which was translated and back translated for translation equivalence (Kumar, 2000), used the language of the respondent (English or Spanish).

From a total of four hundred and eighty-six questionnaires sent (three hundred in the United States and one hundred and eighty-six in Chile), we obtained one hundred and sixty-nine usable surveys (32% from the United States and 39% from Chile), all with valid responses and no missing values. The effective sample size secured 6.5 subjects per variable when only five subjects per variable were needed (Hair et al., 1998, p. 99). The questionnaire included twenty-six questions, and the responses were recorded on a five-point Likert scale with the following possible responses: "of no importance," "of little importance," "of moderate importance," "very important," and "of supreme importance." The scales were then factor analyzed using VARIMAX rotation. The resulting factors were examined using ANOVA.

Anglo-Saxon vs. Latin Cultures

We chose Anglo-Saxon and Latin, to illustrate how the enablers of long-term relationships work when practiced across cultural boundaries. Before we compare the four sets of protocols across those two cultures, we should offer, based on the literature, a brief profile of each culture.

Protestant ethics permeates Anglo-Saxon culture, thus they are characterized by a strong individualism and conservatism (Hickson & Pugh, 1995). Individualist people tend to strive for achievement and personal success; they value individual decisions more than group decisions. Conservative people tend to adopt changes slowly in order to maintain a predictable continuity. Perhaps because of their individualism, Anglo-Saxon people show low power distance (Hofstede, 1980) and prefer a low-context communication that is explicit, direct, and with few subtleties (Hall, 1959). They have a monochronic sense of time.

In contrast, the Latin cultures, which originated in the Roman Empire, are more group-oriented. Despite country-specific differences among the various countries, Latin people are fundamentally collectivist (Hofstede, 1980), as demonstrated by their strong involvement with family and family businesses. In-groups are important in Latin cultures. They exercise a strong influence, derived from their presence in the extensive networks that typify business relations in Latin cultures, over the individual. Like Anglo-Saxon cultures, they also tend to be conservative, adapting to changes in a predictable manner within the context of the past and tradition. Latin cultures tend to be high in power distance (Hofstede, 1980) and prefer more implicit high-context communication, as represented by a language (Spanish) that has an extensive vocabulary (e.g. synonyms) and which relies heavily on non-verbal cues and body language (Hall, 1959). Personal relationships enhance the element of implicitness in the language and can derive their potency from extensive networks of explicit and implicit communication. The time orientation in Latin cultures is polychronic.

Anglo-Saxon vs. Latin Manners

Despite the differences in style between the British and the business people of the United States, the first being the more formal of the two, there is a general sense that Anglo-Saxon business people are more informal than their Latin counterparts (Harris & Moran, 1987). A Latin culture is a mixture of Latin Europeanism and native traditions (Maya, Aztec, and Inca), a blend that understands proper manners and dress style to be indicators of a person's social class, status, and rank (Hall & Hall, 1990). Business must be conducted with politeness, charm, and elegance. Their sense of formality encompasses specific dress codes, clothing styles, and social and table manners. Formal behavior in a Latin culture requires addressing the other person by title, formal name, and using the formal "you" (*usted*), an expression of respect due to differences in organizational rank and age. Thus, the following hypothesis is proposed:

H1. When forging long-term relationships, Anglo-Saxon managers are less formal concerning the business protocols of manners than Latin managers are.

Anglo Saxon vs. Latin Time

The Anglo-Saxon culture's monochronic sense of time and its emphasis on the present encourages an approach to issues and problem-solving based on linear reasoning (Hall & Hall, 1990). Accordingly, Anglo-Saxon people tend to concentrate on one thing at a time, and they dislike having their concentration interrupted. Time is treated as a physical object that can be compartmentalized, a conception that urges respect for schedules. Not surprisingly, Anglo Saxon cultures tend to function only on "formal time." Conversely, the Latin culture tend to have a polychronic orientation (Hall, 1966, 1976), but to varying degrees among Latin Europeans and Latin Americans. Polychronic cultures' multidimensional approach to time is reflected in their institutional use of "formal" time for transportation schedules, schools, and business organizations, while "informal" time structures almost everything else (Hall, 1966). In Latin cultures, issues and problems are approached holistically. Latin people tend not to compartmentalize their time and business relationships as Anglo-Saxons do. Instead, they may perform several overlapping tasks and juggle several relationships at once. In this context, punctuality and deadlines may or may not be important, depending on whether or not individuals have a holistic view of the assignment. Thus, we propose the following hypothesis:

H2. When forging long-term relationships, Anglo-Saxon managers place greater value on the business protocol of time than do Latin managers.

Anglo-Saxon vs. Latin Power Distance

According to Hofstede (1980), Anglo-Saxon cultures are relatively low in power distance. For this reason, competence and personal expertise are valued more than class position or rank; knowledge and skills are more important than who people are (Hickson & Pugh, 1995). Managers are expected to be approachable, to consult their subordinates, and have a participative management style. Nevertheless, Anglo-Saxon organizations are still characterized by a hierarchical structure that is governed by top management and denies representation to lower management ranks and workers.

Latin cultures, unlike their Anglo-Saxon counterparts, vary in power distance (Hofstede, 1980). Latin managers are prone to respect the organizational ranks and status of their clients or prospective clients. When approaching other firms, they prefer to seek counterparts at the same or similar managerial level. Thus, we are led to the following hypothesis:

H3. When forging long-term relationships, Anglo-Saxon managers place less value in the business protocol of power distance than Latin managers do.

Anglo-Saxon vs. Latin Bonding

Because Anglo-Saxon cultures are monochronic and engage in low-context communication that de-emphasizes non-verbal cues and body language, they seem to be uneasy with investing time in the socializing and entertaining that are often necessary preludes to establishing business relationships. U.S. managers feel uneasy mixing business relationships with personal relationships (Hall & Hall, 1990). Thus, bonding with clients or personnel is not likely to be as high a priority for Anglo-Saxon managers as it is for Latin managers when it comes to establishing long-term relationships. The Anglo-Saxon style in a business relationship is skipping the formalities and "getting down to business" as soon as possible. Anglo-Saxon cultures tend to do business with businesses, a level of operation at which personal knowledge of the counterpart is not necessary; a business relationship only is the most desirable way to facilitate communication.

In contrast, the Latin culture's polychronic sense of time and propensity for high-context communication encourages the establishment of more personal relationships among business partners. Latin cultures tend to do business with people rather than businesses. Because of this emphasis on people, there is a need to have this personal knowledge of the counterpart to personalize the business transaction. It is easier to derive a sense of trust and confidence in a long-term commitment from a less formal, more personal relationship than it is from a more structured, formal one. Furthermore, Latin managers usually belong to several in-groups, and the networks formed by these groups can be extensive in depth and scope

(Triandis, Botempo et al., 1988). To become a member of a manager's in-group, it is necessary to develop relationships with its members and thereby earn the trust of the group. Personalization of the relationship usually leads to strong bonding between the interacting business firms, and the relationship created allows trust to develop. This sense of trust enables parties in conflict to resolve their differences through compromise rather than litigation. In this regard it should be noted that in Latin cultures, connotations of conflict of interest are not inherent in the mixing of business and friendship as they are in Anglo-Saxon cultures. In a Latin culture, personal loyalty in business is important, and it is maintained by developing and sustaining personal relationships. Consequently, the following hypothesis is formulated:

H4. In maintaining long-term relationships, Anglo-Saxon managers are less prone to practice the business protocol of bonding than Latin managers are.

RESULTS AND DISCUSSION

Before testing the hypotheses, the results were factor analyzed using principal components to verify whether or not the variables described above are represented in the factors obtained. Principal components are used in exploratory research and need only reliability coefficients above (Churchill, 1999, p. 851; Dillon et al., 1994, pp. 502–503). Principal Component with VARIMAX was used in order to benefit from the orthogonal rotation of factors and the no correlation of factors (Nunnally, 1978, p. 385), as well as to obtain large variances of the square factor loadings so as to achieve results that are more interpretable (Dillon et al., 1994, pp. 502–503). In order to know the differences between U.S. and Chilean managers regarding the use of protocols, we conducted a t-test for the summated variance of each factor.

Table 1 shows the correspondence between protocols and factors. It compares the descriptors derived from the qualitative analysis with the indicators that are significantly loaded in the factors as part of the quantitative analysis. Overall, there is a good fit between the descriptors and the indicators. A similarly good fit can be observed between the protocols identified on the basis of the literature and the quantitative research. The data overwhelmingly reflects what has been identified as protocols and their components. However, we can also observe that the qualitative analysis produced a few more descriptors than the retained indicators in the factor analysis. The two indicators (out of nineteen) that did not load significantly in any factor, or loaded similarly across two or more factors, were excluded, with the exception of "disagreement with supervisor" as explained

Table 2.   Resulting Factors that Reflect Business Protocols.

Indicators	Manners	Time	Power Distance	Bonding
Clothing Style	0.700			
Social Manners	0.630			
Table Manners	0.658			
Punctuality		0.682		
Deadlines		0.753		
Paperwork		0.797		
Titles or first name calling			0.877	
Organizational Ranks			0.691	
Company's Rules			0.792	
Agreement with Supervisor			0.794	
Disagreement with Supervisor			0.549	
Superior's Involvement			0.780	
Cordiality			0.642	
Giving Gifts				0.837
Taking Gifts				0.808
Maintaining Relationships				0.893
Client Maintenance				0.646
Reliability Coefficient	0.7610	0.7015	0.6024	0.6583

below. The consequences of those exclusions and a rationale for the results are discussed next in the corresponding protocol.

Table 2 accounts for the results obtained in the factor analysis and the reliability evaluation. All the loadings obtained are above 0.6 with the exception of "disagreement with supervisor" that shows a loading of 0.549 in Power Distance and a cross-loading of 0.460 in Manners. The decision to retain it in Power Distance was based on theory more than on the small difference between the values. All other loadings are excellent (0.71 and above) or very good (0.63 and above), according to Comrey's and Lee's (1992, p. 243) criteria, and much higher than the minimum acceptable under the 0.3 or above rule (Hair et al., 1998, p. 111).

The range of alpha obtained was 0.60 for the lowest factor (bonding) and 0.76 for the highest factor (time), which is acceptable for exploratory research (Hair et al., 1998, p. 118; Robinson et al., 1991). Thus, all factors are statistically significant, meaning that each factor captured all (or almost all) the elements described as part of a business protocol, which is established by the corresponding cultural norms and followed in the everyday business practices in both Anglo-Saxon and Latin cultures.

Table 3 shows the t-test results. The t-values range between 2.761 and 4.498, and all are significant. A discussion of these findings follows.

Table 3. *t*-Test Results and Hypotheses Testing.

Factor	*t*	df	Sig. (2-tailed)	Hypotheses
Manners	3.183	141.955	0.002	H1. Corroborated
Time	2.761	155.310	0.006	H2. Corroborated
Power Distance	4.498	135.825	0.000	H3. Corroborated
Bonding	5.541	146.288	0.000	H4. Corroborated

Regarding the protocol of manners, Chilean managers are significantly different from U.S. managers ($t = 3.183$, $p = 0.002$), a finding that supports H1. Chilean managers attach more importance to proper social and table manners and to the wearing of appropriate clothing than do their U.S. counterparts. Chileans are attuned to the subtleties of impression management and believe that professionalism is judged partly by how people carry themselves socially and the kind of business attire they wear. One of the Chilean managers interviewed summarized this Latin perspective: "Nothing is written in strict terms, but when someone comes from outside, and he behaves differently or his dress style is different from the environment, the environment automatically forces him to become conscious of this difference – it makes him aware. Unconsciously, he is viewed as lacking professional seriousness. It happens the same with women." Interestingly, private and public organizations in Chile provide uniforms for their operative personnel. A uniform consists of a business suit (for males or females) or three sets of seasonal outfits, perceived as elegant and fashionable, that can be coordinated. The quantitative results are consistent with the literature and the results of the qualitative research. Chilean and U.S. managers place different emphases on manners and clothing style.

"Dress code" was identified as a descriptor in the qualitative research but it was eliminated from the factor of manners because of a low loading in this factor and cross-loading to two other factors. Conceptually, dress code is similar to clothing style, which is already present in the factor. However, we are leaving it to future researchers to explain why dress code did not load significantly in the protocol of manners.

In relation to the protocol of time, both groups of managers are significantly different ($t = 2.761$, $p = 0.006$), thus supporting H2. Polychronic Chilean managers have a more flexible notion of time than their counterparts in the United States, and this conception affects both punctuality and the meeting of deadlines. This is consistent with data obtained from the interviews, in which Chilean managers indicated that a window of twenty minutes (arriving up to twenty minutes late) is still viewed as being on time for a meeting. To monochronic U.S. managers, being punctual and meeting deadlines indicate the sense of responsibility and professionalism a person feels. Thus, their window of tolerance for lateness is very narrow. As a manager in the United States said, "Our biggest concern is not to be late when we meet the clients because we are using valuable clients' time, and their time is working for them. We do not want to be disrespectful."

Regarding the protocol of power distance, Chilean managers also are significantly different from American managers ($t = 4.498$, $p = 0.000$), thus supporting H3. Following organizational rules and respecting the differences in organizational ranks within their own company and with prospective clients is more important to Chilean managers than it is to their U.S. counterparts. The Chilean managers interviewed indicated that it was best to approach a prospective firm at the peer level, or at most, just one level higher than their own rank. For them, negotiations must move upward, level by level through the management hierarchy. Top management gets involved only to finalize details. One Chilean manager drew an analogy between a chess game and the strategy for negotiating a managerial hierarchy: "Generally, the relationships are at the same levels. It is rare that they would jump levels. That is, one level could be jumped, but jumping two or three levels is very rare. Nobody comes to speak with the general manager of a company. I will say that is impossible." U.S. managers, however, prefer to contact the prospective client at the highest level possible in the firm. As one U.S. manager indicated, "In sales, you want to get to the decision maker, so I don't think anyone is worried about levels. I want to know who the decision maker is, and I try to reach that person."

Regarding the supervisor's involvement in an employee's work and potential disagreements with the supervisor, it is more important to the Chilean manager than it is to the U.S. managers to have the supervisor involved in working decisions, as Chileans feel uncomfortable disagreeing with the supervisor. Consistent with a high power distance, Chilean managers consider it important to address their clients at first by their last name or title, and then moving to a first-name basis. They will wait for an explicit invitation to use the informal "you." Conversely, managers from the United States indicated that they prefer to move to a first-name basis immediately or within the first ten minutes of the meeting, and they are willing to do so without an invitation to make the switch.

"Cordiality" is considered a sign of respect for another person, but it also reflects the gray shades of power distance, as exemplified by Chilean and U.S. managers. It is more important to Chilean managers to conduct business with cordiality than it is to their U.S. counterparts. Chilean managers manifested discomfort when dealing with open disagreements or when being openly challenged at meetings. They consider these behaviors very rude. U.S. managers are more tolerant of disagreements and having their opinions challenged in meetings. They see the contribution that such behavior makes in brainstorming sessions aimed at securing better outcomes. These results are consistent with what Triandis et al. (1984) describe as the Simpatía Script, and Hickson and Pugh (1995) assert that Latin managers do business with grace and deal with disagreements less directly than do their U.S. counterparts.

Regarding the protocol of bonding, both groups are significantly different ($t = 5.541, p = 0.0000$), a result which supports H4. Both Chilean and U.S. managers share the view that establishing and maintaining relationships with customers is necessary, but establishing long-term personal relationships is more important to Chilean managers than it is to their counterparts in the United States. Not surprisingly, then, the managers from the two cultures differ in the way they believe such relationships are to be achieved. Overall, business relationships in the United States have clearer and narrower boundaries than those in Chile. In the United States, a business relationship can be established without involving a personal relationship, so personal friendships with clients are avoided as much as possible, mainly because of the perception that a personal relationship between managers and clients may generate conflicts of interest when it comes to making tough business decisions.

The remarks of one bank manager illustrate the ambivalence U.S. managers feel toward developing more personal relationships with clients: "We have a relationship manager that keeps information on customers. In a big company, you really have to operate that way, because, if the relationship sours, you do not want people from other parts of the bank trying to help the relationship. If the client suddenly is not paying his or her loans, you do not want to be selling other credit products. Everything goes through this relationship manager." Conversely, business contracts or business negotiations in Chile are usually preceded by an informal relationship with the prospective client. Moreover, business relationships in Chile have a broader scope and usually involve personal friendships.

Nowhere is this difference in attitudes toward personal relationships in business more apparent than in gift-giving, a traditional practice in both Chile and the United States. It is more important to the Chilean manager than it is to the United States manager to exchange gifts as a demonstration of personal and business appreciation, for this personal expression, to a Chilean manager, is an important element in cementing and sustaining long-term personal relationships in a business environment. This difference in attitude toward gifts is frequently, as the U.S. manager quoted above indicates, a concern that personal relationships can interfere with sound business decisions. And there is probably also some fear among U.S. managers that gifts can be easily misconstrued, causing a hapless manager to run afoul of regulations governing gifts. Clients and managers in both cultures are acutely aware that the gifts given and received need to be recognized by everyone as gifts and not bribes. The level of concern manifests itself in attendant regulating mechanisms. The Chilean managers interviewed indicated that even though Chile lacks national regulations governing gift-exchange such as the U.S. Foreign Corrupt Practice Act, most Chilean firms do have rules regulating the value of gifts, most of which are office-related items or morally neutral items such as books and CDs. It would be difficult to see these items as bribes, and in the event they might be, Chilean managers have mechanisms for distributing these gifts to parties not involved in business decisions.

Cultivating customer loyalty is the goal of establishing and maintaining long-term relationships for both groups. However, each group nurture feelings of loyalty in customers through different processes. Chilean managers create, within a broader scope of business relationships, a sense of loyalty by cultivating friendships with the clients. U.S. managers create a sense of loyalty by forging an enduring and stable business relationship which is defined more narrowly so as to exclude personal friendships with clients.

Loyalty is present in Table 1, but as a descriptor only, and not as an indicator because it is similarly cross-loaded in two factors, bonding and power distance. Consequently, loyalty was eliminated as a separate indicator of bonding. Loyalty, however, is reflected to some extent by the other indicators of bonding, gift exchange, maintaining relationships, and client maintenance. One of the expected outcomes of exchanging gifts and maintaining relationships is, not surprisingly, loyalty.

In sum, Chilean managers emphasize business relationships whose boundaries are broad enough to accommodate personal friendship. Trust and commitment are achieved as a result of long-term personal relationships that are devoid of perceived conflicts of interests. In contrast, managers in the United States emphasize business relationships that have well defined, narrow boundaries that allow only business interrelations and prohibit personal friendship. They believe that friendship implicitly carries responsibilities and obligations that can create conflicts of interest. In this context, trust and commitment are achieved, but as a consequence of prolonged business relationships themselves, not as a by-product of cultivating personal friendships.

SUMMARY AND CONCLUSIONS

The main objective of this paper is to advance research on the identification and description of the primary steps that lead to the formation and maintenance of relationship marketing in cross-cultural business. To achieve our objective, we first identified the communication difficulties in generating and maintaining long-term relationships in bicultural or multicultural settings. We then developed the building blocks, or enablers, that are needed to form and maintain enduring business relationships. Finally, we illustrated what we are suggesting is the process by describing the use of enablers in contrasting cultures, the Anglo-Saxon and the Latin.

The first challenge we identified was the establishing of effective communication across cultures. We wanted to know what mechanisms business people of different cultures utilized to establish successful communication and develop long-term relationships. The second challenge we identified dealt with the process of communication itself and describing the nature and scope of the enablers of long-term relationships between people of different cultures.

The enablers used protocols, or scripts, to cultivate and maintain long-term relationships. The protocols that help the formation of long-term relationships across cultures relate to: (a) manners as expressed in social and table manners, and clothing style; (b) the value of time as represented by punctuality for appointments and meeting deadlines; and (c) the obligations due to differential power (power distance) and status as symbolized by the preferences in the use of first name and the scope of disagreement with supervisors. The protocol that helps maintain long-term relationships is bonding through the use of gift exchanges and the maintenance of relationships and clients, with or without personal friendship.

The use of contrasting cultures, Anglo-Saxon and Latin, uncovered additional challenges in the identification and development of adequate enablers in the establishment or maintenance of long-term relationships and exemplified two distinct ways of responding to them. Both groups of managers use all the protocols and their components as enablers; however, each group, despite apparent similarities, uses the protocols in its own way. The inclination towards individualism or collectivism, inherited from their corresponding societies, permeates not only each culture's business interactions, but also the manner in which people from a culture approach life generally.

Both cultures attach different degrees of importance to the enablers that either facilitate the formation of or contribute to the maintenance of long-term relationships. Regarding the protocol of manners, for example, Chilean managers assigned far more importance to impression management, social and table etiquette, and the use of last names and titles. Often these protocols become part of the criteria used to judge the degree of professionalism of a businessperson. Conversely, U.S. managers are comfortable with a more informal approach to social manners and clothing style.

There are also differences with respect to the protocol of time. Polychronic-oriented Chilean managers strive for punctuality, but they have a somewhat more casual approach to schedules and deadlines than their monochronic-oriented counterparts in the United States, who have a linear approach to time, so much so that their lives become compartmentalized in defined sectors. For U.S. managers, punctuality and respect for deadlines are significant among the criteria they use to judge the degree of professionalism of a businessperson. Apparently, the two cultures have different sets of time-related criteria for judging professionalism. In cross-cultural relations, such differences can generate misunderstandings and misinterpretations, unless both sides of the relationship are aware of the cultural dissimilarities in using time as a business protocol.

The cross-cultural differences regarding power distance are also paramount. Chilean managers approach a targeted business firm at a peer level. They develop the relationship upward from that point on, level by level, obtaining commitments from the people at one level before advancing to the next. They are painstaking in their approach because each level has the authority to terminate the negotiation. Managers in the United States, on the other hand, approach the targeted business firm at the highest decision-making point. The authority in U.S. businesses is concentrated at the top of the organization, while in Chile the authority is spread throughout the different levels of the firm.

Furthermore, the willingness to invest the time in a negotiation is also different in both cultures. Chilean managers are far more willing to invest time in a meticulous process, whereas managers from the United States consider step-by-step negotiations an unnecessary expenditure not only their time but also their clients' valuable time. A negotiation takes a long time when it moves slowly from level to level up the hierarchical ladder than it does when taken directly to the top decision maker. Yet, the commitment obtained from the lower managerial levels along the longer route can make the decisions more palatable to the rest of the corporation, whereas a weakness in the negotiation resulting from a lack of commitment on the part of lower level managers when the shorter route is taken must be remedied by promoting and/or selling the decision to the rest of the company, which may or may not embrace a decision made only at the top.

Finally, both cultures are essentially different regarding the protocol of bonding, particularly in the way they approach the cultivation of long-term loyalty. For Chilean managers, business relationships are defined within broad boundaries so that informal relations such as friendship can be included. Friendship personalizes the business relations beyond formal communications and creates a set of obligations and responsibilities that are beyond the strictly defined business boundaries, but which are necessary to form and maintain long business relationships. Informal arrangements that are not part of a business relationship, particularly friendships, must be avoided by United States managers because they can create conflicts of interest when making business decisions. Chilean managers, being from a high-context culture, feel comfortable with the reciprocity of responsibilities and obligations that inject an element of humanness in the business relationship, whereas United States managers, being from a low-context culture, prefer to stay legalistic and limit the relationship to written contracts or other instruments that govern the business relationship.

Knowing the cross-cultural differences in the business protocols of manners, time, power distance, and bonding can help managers from one culture successfully approach their counterparts from another culture. Moreover, such knowledge is essential to the formation of long-term relationships and, with good reason, in their maintenance. In practical terms, the use of known protocols of manners, time, power distance, and bonding is particularly important to achieve the following: (a) avoiding cultural mistakes in relating to business people that belong to different cultures; (b) using the appropriate instruments to develop long-term relationships across cultures; and (c) becoming effective in the maintenance of long-term cross-cultural relationships.

Limitations and Future Research

Although the resulting factors reflecting the protocols are robust and meaningful, two indicators, dress code and loyalty, did not load significantly in their corresponding factors and cross-loaded to other factors. Thus, further exploration regarding these indicators is needed with new samples in different industries. Also clarification is needed regarding the indicator disagreement with supervisor. Does it reveal manners or power distance? Theory suggests it is power distance, but the data supports a linkage to manners as well. New data sets can help clarifying this dilemma.

All factors should be examined in various industries to make sure that they are general enough to allow for broader predictions. Similarly, other cultural groups such as European, Asian or African should be compared regarding the protocols they use and the way they use them. If a slower process has to be followed, new cross-country comparisons can still be pursued in order to increase the generalizability of our findings.

REFERENCES

Axtell, R. E. (1985). *Do's and taboos around the world*. Compiled by the Parker Pen Company. New York: John Wiley and Sons.
Barlow, R. G. (1992). Relationship marketing: The ultimate in customer services. *Retail Control*, 29–37.

Berger, C., & Calabrese, R. (1975). Some explorations in initial interaction and beyond. *Human Communication Research, 1*, 99–112.

Berry, L. (1983). Relationship marketing. In: G. Upah (Ed.), *Emerging Perspectives on Service Marketing* (pp. 25–38). Chicago: American Marketing Association.

Brislin, R. W. (1981). *Cross-cultural encounters. Face-to-face interaction.* New York: Pergamon Press.

Burgoon, J. K., Buller, D. B., & Woodal, W. G. (1996). *Non-verbal communication. The unspoken dialogue* (2nd ed.). New York: McGraw-Hill Co.

Churchill, G. A. (1999). *Marketing research: Methodological foundations* (7th ed.). New York: Dryden Press.

Comrey, A. L., & Lee, H. B. (1992). *A first course in factor analysis* (2nd ed.). London: Lawrence Erlbaum Associates, Publishers.

Copeland, L., & Griggs, L. (1985). *Going international.* New York: Random House.

Dillon, W. (1976). *Gifts and nations.* New Jersey: Prentice-Hall.

Dillon, W. R., Madden, T. J., & Firtle, N. H. (1994). *Marketing research in a marketing environment* (3rd ed.). Boston: Irwin.

Frazier, G. L., Gill, J., & Kale, S. (1989). Dealer dependence levels and reciprocal action in a channel of distribution in a developing country. *Journal of Marketing, 53*(1), 50–69.

Ganesan, S. (1993). Negotiation strategies and the nature of channel relationships. *Journal of Marketing Research, 30*, 183–202.

Goffman, E. (1959). *The presentation of self in everyday life.* Garden City: Doubleday.

Goffman, E. (1976). *Interaction ritual: Essays on face-to-face behavior.* Garden City: Doubleday.

Gordon, I. (2000). Organizing for relationship marketing. In: A. Parvatiyar (Ed.), *Handbook of Relationship Marketing* (pp. 505–523). London: Sage.

Graham, J. (1985). Cross-cultural marketing negotiations: A laboratory experiment. *Marketing Science, 4*(Spring), 130–146.

Gudykunst, W., & Lim, T. (1986). A perspective for the study of intergroup communicator style. In: W. Gudykunst (Ed.), *Intergroup Communication.* London: Edward Arnold.

Gummesson, E. (1987). The new marketing: Developing long-term interactive relationships. *Long-Range Planning, 20*(4), 10–20.

Hair, J. F. E. A. R., Tathan, R. L., & Black, W. C. (1998). *Multivariate data analysis* (5th ed.). Upper Saddle River, NJ: Prentice Hall.

Hall, E. T. (1959). *The silent language.* New York: Doubleday.

Hall, E. T. (1966). *The hidden dimension.* New York: Doubleday.

Hall, E. T. (1976). *Beyond culture.* New York: Doubleday.

Hall, E. T. (1982). *The dance of life. The other dimension of time.* New York: Doubleday.

Hall, R. H. (1991). *Organizations: Structures, processes and outcomes* (5th ed.). Englewood Cliff, NJ: Prentice Hall.

Hall, E. T., & Hall, M. R. (1990). *Understanding cultural differences.* Maine: Intercultural Press.

Harris, P. R., & Moran, R. T. (1987). *Managing cultural differences.* Houston: Gulf Publishing Co.

Hickson, D. J., & Pugh, D. D. (1995). *Management worldwide. The impact of societal culture on organizations around the world.* London: Penguin Books.

Hincks, W. (2002). *An evaluation of lawlike generalization in relationship marketing: Method and application.* Unpublished Ph. D. Dissertation, University of Texas – Pan American, Edinburg.

Hofstede, G. (1980). *Culture's consequences international differences in work-related values.* Newbury Park: Sage.

Hui, C. H., & Triandis, H. (1986). Individualism-collectivism: A study of cross-cultural research. *Journal of Cross-Cultural Psychology, 17*, 225–248.

Hunt, S. D., & Morgan, R. M. (1994). Relationship marketing in an era of network competition. *Marketing Management*, *3*(1), 19–28.

Kendon, A., & Ferber, A. (1973). A description of some human greetings. In: J. H. Crook (Ed.), *Comparative Ecology and Behavior of Primates*. London: Academic Press.

Knapp, M., & Hall, J. (1997). *Non-verbal communication in human interaction* (4th ed.). New York: Harcourt Brace College Publishers.

Kumar, V. (2000). *International marketing research*. New Jersey: Prentice Hall.

Laurent, A. (1983). The cultural diversity of western conception of management. *International Studies of Management and Organization*, *13*(1), 75–96.

Levine, R., & Wolff, E. (1985). Social time: The heartbeat of culture. *Psychology Today*, 28–30.

Malandro, L. A., Barker, L., & Barker, D. A. (1989). *Non-verbal communication* (Vol. 2). New York: McGraw-Hill.

Morgan, R. M. (2000). Relationship marketing and marketing strategy. In: A. Parvatiyar (Ed.), *Handbook of Relationship Marketing* (pp. 481–504). London: Sage.

Nunnally, J. C. (1978). *Psychometric theory*. New York: McGraw-Hill.

O'Hara-Devereaux, M., & Johansen, R. (1994). *Globalwork. Bridging distance, culture, and time*. San Francisco: Jossey-Bass.

Parasuraman, A., Berry, L. L., & Zeithmal, V. A. (1991). Understanding customer expectations of service. *Sloan Management Review*, *32*(3), 39–48.

Reichheld, F. F. (1996). *The loyalty effect: The hidden force behind growth, profits, and lasting values*. Boston: Harvard Business School Press.

Ridgeway, C. L., Berger, J., & Smith, L. (1985). Non-verbal cues and status: An expectation states approach. *American Journal of Sociology*, *90*, 955–978.

Robinson, J. P., Shaver, P. R., & Wringhtsman, L. S. (1991). Criteria for scale selection and evaluation. In: L. S. Wringhtsman (Ed.), *Measures of Personality and Social Psychological Attitudes*. San Diego: Academic Press.

Rosenber, L. J., & Czepiel, J. A. (1984). A marketing approach to customers: A pilot study. *Journal of Consumer Marketing*, *1*(2), 45–51.

Sheth, J., & Parvatiyar, A. (Eds) (2000). *Handbook of relationship marketing* (1st ed.) London: Sage Publications.

Singh, T. (1995). Measurement issues in cross-cultural research. *Journal of International Business Studies*, *26*(3), 597–619.

Sisoda, R. S., & Wolfe, D. B. (2000). Information technology. In: A. Parvatiyar (Ed.), *Handbook of Relationship Marketing* (pp. 525–563). London: Sage.

Tayeb, M. H. (1992). *The global business environment. An introduction*. Newbury Park: Sage.

Tayeb, M. H. (1996). *The management of a multicultural workforce*. New York: John Wiley & Sons.

Triandis, H., Botempo, R., Villareal, M., Asai, M., & Lucca, N. (1988). Individualism and collectivism: Cross-cultural perspectives on self-in-group relationships. *Journal of Personality and Social Psychology*, *54*(2), 323–338.

Triandis, H., Brislin, R. W., & Hui, C. H. (1988). Cross-cultural training across the individualism collectivism divide. *International Journal of Intercultural Relations*, *12*, 269–289.

Triandis, H., Marin, G., Lisansky, J., & Betancourt, H. (1984). Simpatia as a cultural script of hispanics. *Journal of Personality and Social Psychology*, *47*(6), 1363–1375.

Varadarajan, P. R., & Cunningham, M. H. (1995). Strategic alliances: A synthesis of conceptual foundations. *Journal of the Academy of Marketing Science*, *23*(4), 282–296.

Weitz, B. A., & Jap, S. D. (1995). Relationship marketing and distribution channels. *Journal of the Academy of Marketing Science*, *23*(4), 305–320.

SUBJECT INDEX